SAND GULL

沙

鷗

SAND GULL

Poems of Du Fu

Volume 2

TRANSLATED BY
Kwan-Hung Chan

Copyright © 2021 by Kwan-Hung Chan

ISBN 978-1-4999-0725-4

Printed in the United States of America

Published May 2021

Contents

2. POEMS NOT IN CHRONOLOGY ..265

xvi

PREFACE

Du Fu (712-770) showed affection for gulls in his poems. This sentiment was shared by Li Bai (701-762) when he wrote "The moon in-stream looks white under a clear sky. With my serenity at heart, a sea gull can identify" 天清江月白，心靜海鷗知 According to Liezi, a 4th century Daoist text on philosophy, the gulls in a parable can read the human mind, especially schemes.

This volume covers a good number of verses of Du Fu written in Kuizhou 夔州 (Present day Chongqing 重慶) when he settled down in his mid fifties as a gentleman farmer and his poetic skill reached maturity.

In 766 at Kuizhou, Du Fu produced his most famous set of eight poems: Autumn Inspiration 秋興八首, showcasing his impeccable prosodic skill in antithetical couplets 對仗 with unparalleled density and imagery. According to his critics, the flow of language in his lines offers swiftness of rhythm rarely found.

In his days as a refugee from the An Lushan Rebellion (755-763), Du Fu had two benefactors: Military Commander Yan Wu 嚴武 (726-765) in Chengdu and Governor Bo Maolin 柏茂琳 in Kuizhou. Both respected him as a friend and poet. He was offered a job in the local government in both places.

Because of wars and palace politics, Du Fu was disappointed that he could not hold a high-ranking position in the capital. One of his personal tragedies was the death of his son due to starvation. He wrote poems as he traveled for shelter and ended quite a few with laments on his own health and fate. There is a profound sense of pathos expressed.

His writings on the trips were necessary and therapeutic to him, as shown in his words: "Writing poetry from my heart consoles this wanderer as I often move about, sick and distressed" 緣情慰飄蕩，抱疾屢遷移 However, he did not always have sympathizers.

In the end, Du Fu was tired of his lifestyle with these lines: "Tired of writing poems as I travel on land and water, I can still pen my thoughts if I try" 采詩倦跋涉，載筆尚可記 When Du Fu was about fifty-five years old, his experience in the capacity of a gentleman farmer in River West 瀼西 allowed him to broaden his narrative scope in areas of harvesting, weeding and other social activities and write with more hope.

In 768, Du Fu began his voyage home after having a boat built for that purpose. He wanted to meet his long lost relatives again some of whom held administrative positions in nearby counties or villages. In 770, at Tanzhou, due to failing health, he died in his boat without reaching home.

As a poet in a life of penury and itinerancy, Du Fu was not greatly appreciated by his contemporaries. Bai Juyi (772-846)白居易 was the first poet to recognize and publicize the worth of his poems. His good friend Yuan Zhen (779-831) 元稹, a colleague and famed poet, held the same conviction of the need of verses to protest social evils.

In 813, at the request of Du Siye, grandson of Du Fu, Yuan Zhen wrote a grave inscription for Du Fu. In the preface on the epitaph, he indicated that as poets, in areas of narrative scope and prosodic technique, Du Fu is way above Li Bai. This is one of several schools of thoughts in comparing the two poets.

From the Song Dynasty onwards, Du Fu was much admired He is now known as China's Shakespeare and hailed as Poet-Historian and Poet-Sage.

Scholars of Du Fu through the centuries have linked some of his poems to particular years based on the contents and his own notes. With exceptions, many of his poems included in this volume are less well-known and have not been assigned a date. Based on clues from his activities, geographical locations and names of people mentioned, I have grouped his later poems under several broad periods of time: 760-764 Chengdu Years, 765-767 Kuizhou Years and 768-770

Voyage Home. Other poems on nature or non-specific events are listed under "Poems Not in Chronology", in alphabetical order by title. In a few cases, the archaic Chinese characters used are replaced by their modern and variant forms.

The 286 poems translated in this book represent a fraction of his corpus of one thousand four hundred poems. I would like to thank my friends and relatives who have helped me in this project.

1. POEMS IN CHRONOLOGY

Year 745

劉九法曹鄭瑕丘石門宴集

秋水清無底，蕭然靜客心。掾農乘逸
興，鞍馬去相尋。能吏逢聯壁，華筵
直一金。晚來橫吹好，泓下亦龍吟。

Feast at Stonegate Mountain Hosted by Judge Liu, the Ninth, and Zheng of Xiaqiu

The quietness soothes the hearts of the
  guests.
Autumn waters look limpid all the way.
Government employees with refined
  tastes,
On horseback, seek such scenery far
  away.

Like linked jade discs, you are two able
    officials.
For the grand feast, it takes a pot of gold
    to pay.
Flood dragons deep down also chant
To our fine flute notes, late in the day.

Year 753

送高三十五書記十五韻

I

崆峒小麥熟，且願休王師。請公問主
將，焉用窮荒為。飢鷹未飽肉，側翅
隨人飛。高生跨鞍馬，有似幽并兒。
脫身薄尉中，始與捶楚辭。借問今何
官，觸熱向武威。答云一書記，所愧
國士知。人實不易知，更須慎其儀。

十年去幕府，自可持旌麾。此行既特
達，足以慰所思。男兒功名遂，亦在
老大時。常恨結歡淺，各在天一涯。
又與參與商，慘慘中腸悲。驚風吹鴻
鵠，不得相追隨。黃塵翳沙漠，念子
何當歸。邊城有餘力，早寄從軍詩。

Seeing off Secretary Gao Shi, the Thirty-fifth in Fifteen Couplets

I

On Mount Kongtong, the wheat is ripe.
That the king's army would rest, I pray.
Let me ask the commanding general:
What is the use of going to the wilds far
away?

Starving hawks, without their fill of
meat,
Follow people and tilt their wings in
flight.

Like young warriors of You and Bing,
On horseback, Mister Gao shows fight.

From clerkship or punishments used
    as a sheriff,
You have just been free.
Now, to bear the heat of Wuwei, at the
    new post,
Which official is willing, I beg to query.

"As a secretary recognized by a top
    official,
The honor is too much" you did reply.
It is really hard to understand people.
Minding your manners is what you
    should try.

II

After ten years in the headquarters,
As a leader, you can play your part.
This trip, promising of special success,
Is enough to comfort my heart.

Fame and glory

Tend to be what older people can get.
Since we are at different ends of the sky,
That our joyous unions are brief, I often
  regret.

Like Shen and Shang, stars that never
  meet,
My heart is in sorrow.
A frightful wind splits wild swans,
Giving no chance to catch up and follow.

A yellow sandstorm veils deserts.
When is your returning day?
With energy to spare in your frontier
  town,
Send me a poem on expeditions without
  delay.

送人從軍

弱水應無地，陽關已近天。今君度沙
磧，累月斷人煙。好武寧論命，封侯
不計年。馬寒防失道，雪沒錦鞍韉。

Seeing Someone off on an Expedition

There should be no land by River Ruo.
Near the sky, through Yang Pass one
   can go.
Now you will cross the deserts,
Where, for months, chimney smoke
   from homes does not show.
Military careerists do not discuss fate.
After bestowed titles, they always
   follow.
Your horse, in the cold, can prevent
   getting lost on the way,
To the height of your brocade saddle
   cover, with snow.

送遠

帶甲滿天地，胡為君遠行。親朋盡一
哭，鞍馬去孤城。草木歲月晚，關河
霜雪清。別離已昨日，因見古人情。

Seeing Someone off afar

Armored soldiers are everywhere.
Why do you go far away?
Friends and relatives all weep,
As you gallop for a lone city on your
    way.
Clear frost and snow cover pass and
    river.
Late in the year, plants are in decay.
I share the sorrow of an ancient poet in
    "Parting for a Long Time".
The pain will stay and grow after you
    left yesterday.

遣憤

聞道花門將，論功未盡歸。自從收帝
里，誰復總戎機。蜂蠆終懷毒，雷霆
可震威。莫令鞭血地，再濕漢臣衣。

Expressing my Outrage

I have heard the Uighur generals
Have not all returned after the fight.
Ever since we retook the capital,
Who makes the overall war decisions
	again?
Like hornets and scorpions, nomad
	rebels are ultimately poisonous.
Like peals of thunder, we can show our
	might.
Do not let another Uighur chief do
	flogging
And cover the robe of our envoy with

a blood stain.

留花門

北門天驕子，飽肉氣勇決。高秋馬肥
健，挾矢射漢月。自古以爲患，詩人
厭薄伐。修德使其來，羈縻固不絕。
胡為傾國至，出入暗金闕。

Keeping People from Huamen Mountain

Heaven's favored sons from the north,
　　well-fed in meat,
Let their energy and combat valor show.
In cloudless fall, on fat, strong horses,
Uighurs help us fight invaders with bow
　　and arrow.
This poet loathes small, indecisive wars,
Which lead to troubles since ages ago.
Our culture and ethics draw them in.
Efforts to tame brutes are not let go.
How come the whole nation arrived?

On our empire, the traffic casts a
  shadow.

九日曲江

綴席茱萸好，浮舟菡萏衰。季秋時欲
半，九日意兼悲。江水清源曲，荊門
此路疑。晚來高興盡，搖蕩菊花期。

On the Double Ninth Day at Qujiang Waterway

Prickly Ash adorns our mats well.
We drift in a boat with lotuses in decay.
On the Double Ninth Day, I have an
  added tinge of sadness,
In late fall, with boating going halfway.
At the source, this limpid river bends,
But to Jingmen, it seems to be the way.
In this season of chrysanthemums,
  rocked by the boat,
I am in utmost joy, late in the day.

日暮

日落風亦起，城頭烏尾訛。黃雲高未動，白水已揚波。羌婦語還笑，胡兒行且歌。將軍別換馬，夜出擁雕戈。

Twilight

Atop the city wall, tails of crows do not
    align.
Winds rise at twilight.
White billows have already started on
    waters.
A yellow sandstorm hangs still at a
    height.
Nomad men walk and sing.
Qiang women talk and laugh in delight.
The departing general changes his horse,
Holding a carved pike to leave at night.

Year 759

寒硤

行邁日悄悄，山谷勢多端。雲門轉絕
岸，積阻霾天寒。寒硤不可度，我實
衣裳單。況當仲冬交，沍沿增波瀾。
野人尋煙語，行人傍水餐。此生免荷
殳，未敢辭路難。

Cold Valley

It looks drearier as I travel each day.
Hills and valleys look diverse in the
　　land's lay.
Like doors in clouds, rocks stand at the
　　bend of steep cliffs.
The mass blocks chilly mist on its way.

My clothing is really thin.
The cold valley cannot be crossed.
Moreover, it is mid-winter now.

To follow the stream, by big waves I
  shall be tossed.

Rustics seek a fire with smoke and talk.
Beside waters, travelers dine.
If in this life I can avoid shouldering
  weapons for war,
The hardship of wandering I dare not
  decline.

積草嶺

連峰積長陰，白日遞隱見。颼颼林響
交，慘慘石狀變。山分積草嶺，路異
明水縣。旅泊吾道窮，衰年歲時倦。
卜居尚百里，休駕投諸彥。邑有佳主
人，情如已會面。來書語絕妙，遠客
驚深眷。食蕨不願餘，茅茨眼中見。

Grassy Ridge

It is cloudy everywhere on joined peaks.

The bright sun is in and out of sight.
Sadly the shapes of rocks change.
In the forest, winds with swishing
  sounds unite.

Another trail leads to Bright Water
  County.
From Grassy Ridge, different hillocks
  unfold.
A regular wanderer, I reach a roadblock
  of my life,
Often feeling tired as I get old.

To stop my ride and join some refined
  people,
I need to get to my lodging, a hundred
  miles apart.
There is a hospitable host in town.
His sentiment is like that of a reunited
  friend at heart.

A frightened traveler afar really holds
  dear
The letter of invitation, superbly written,
  coming through.

I wish for no more than a diet for
 recluses
And a thatched hut coming in view.

夏夜歎

永日不可暮，炎蒸毒我腸。安得萬里
風，飄飄吹我裳。昊天出華月，茂林
延疏光。仲夏苦夜短，開軒納微涼。
虛明見纖毫，羽蟲亦飛揚。物情無巨
細，自適固其常。念彼荷戈士，窮年
守邊疆。何由一洗濯，執熱互相望。
竟夕擊刁斗，喧聲連萬方。青紫雖被
體，不如早還鄉。北城悲笳發，鸛鶴
號且翔。況復煩促倦，激烈思時康。

Sighs over a Summer Night

With a torrid haze that poisons my guts,
The lasting sun never yields to twilight.
How can my robe be fluttered by wind,
From countless miles to this site?

The lovely moon from the summer sky,
Past a thicket, sends sparse moonlight.
Nights are painfully short in mid-
summer.
My open door will let in cool air,
however slight.

One can see fine filaments in the semi-
darkness.
Birds and insects are in flight.
Living things, big or small, can adapt
To nature for what is regular and right.

I think of soldiers all year with pikes,
Guarding the frontiers tight.
How can we not help out in danger, like
someone holding a hot object,
When water can make the pain light?

The uproar of victory reaches endless
regions,
With the beating of drum and gong all
night.
Though the wearing of purple and green

marks nobility,
It pales compared with returning home,
  to my insight.

North of the wall, cheerless notes of
  reed pipes begin.
Storks and cranes cry, soaring to a
  height.
What is more, worries tire me fast.
I wish hard for peace to be in sight.

夏日歎

夏日出東北，陵天經中街。朱光徹厚
地，鬱蒸何由開。上蒼久無雷，無乃
號令乖。雨降不濡物，良田起黃埃。
飛鳥苦熱死，池魚涸其泥。萬人尚流
冗，舉目唯蒿萊。至今大河北，化作
虎與豺。浩蕩想幽薊，王師安在哉。
對食不能餐，我心殊未諧。眇然貞觀
初，難與數子偕。

Sighs over the Summer Sun

The summer sun comes out to the
    northeast,
Crossing the sky for a middle lane.
Red beams fully cover the thick earth.
Evaporation is not what we can obtain.

For long, Heaven has not thundered.
It must be due to the misrule of the
    sovereign.
Yellow dust rises from good fields.
Things do not get wet after any rain.

Fish in ponds dry up in mud.
Birds in flight die from the heat in pain.
Countless people become outlaws.
Only weeds are seen in the terrain.

By now, north of the big river, good
    citizens rebel,
Acting like tigers and jackals in our
    domain.
Where is the imperial army?
I think of the vast bases at You and Ji

that rebels gain.

I cannot eat the food before me.
Efforts for my peace of mind are in vain.
It is hard to be in the midst of several
  able ministers again,
From the dim past, of the early
  Zhengguan reign.

法鏡寺

身危適他州。勉強終勞苦。神傷山行
深，愁破崖寺古。嬋娟碧蘚淨，蕭撼
寒籜聚。回回山根水，冉冉松上雨。
洩雲蒙清晨，初日翳復吐。朱甍半光
炯，戶牖粲可數。挂策忘前期，出蘿
已亭午。冥冥子規叫，微徑不復取。

The Temple of the Dharma Mirror

In danger, I travel to another county,
Facing hardships with patience, after

toil and pain.
Deep in the hills, my spirit breaks.
An old temple at the cliff lifts it again.

Clean green lichens look lovely.
Wind-battered bamboo sheaths gather in
the chill.
Above pines, rain goes on and on.
Waters twist and turn at the base of the
hill.

The early dawn sky is under trickling
clouds.
Later, the first sunbeams break through.
Red roof tiles are half lit.
Doors and windows come in full view.

I lean on my staff, with my trip ahead
forgotten.
Emerging from vines, I find it is already
midday.
When cuckoos call in the dark,
I no longer take a byway.

Year 760-764

将晓二首，其一

石城除擊柝，鐵鎖欲開關。鼓角悲荒
塞，星河落曙山。巴人常小梗，蜀使
動無還。垂老孤帆色，飄飄犯百蠻。

Approaching Dawn, no.1

The sound of watch clappers ends at
stone walls.
With iron chains off, they are about to
open the gate.
The Milky Way is gone beyond dawn
hills.
The deserted frontier, with bugle and
drum, is in a cheerless state.
Envoys sent to Shu never return,
To settle small social issues that Ba
people often create.
An aging trespasser, adrift with a lone

sail,
To the many barbarian tribes here, I
cannot relate.

弊廬遣興奉寄嚴公

野水平橋路，春沙映竹村。風輕粉蝶
喜，花暖蜜蜂暄。把酒宜深酌，題詩
好細論。府中瞻暇日，江上憶詞源。
跡忝朝廷舊，情依節制尊。還思長車
轍，恐避席為門。

**At my Worn Thatched Cottage,
Expressing my Inspiration:
Respectfully Sent to Lord Yan**

This nameless river rises to the bridge
and road.
Onto bamboos of the village in spring,
sands reflect sunlight.
Honey bees buzz loudly amid warm
flowers.

Powdery butterflies look cheerful in
　　wind that is light.

It is proper to be unreserved with wine
　　when I drink,
And good to be detailed in prosody as I
　　write.
In your headquarters, you look forward
　　to days of rest.
By the river, I recall your poetic insight.

Ashamed to be an old colleague of yours
　　in the palace,
I go by rules and respect what is right.
A poor man of Han with a mat as his
　　door got visits by dignitaries.
Your coming to see me at my humble
　　home clears my fright.

嚴鄭公宅同詠竹 （得香字）

綠竹半含籜，新梢纔出牆。色侵書帙
晚，陰過酒樽涼。雨洗娟娟淨，風吹
細細香。但令無剪伐，會見拂雲長。

At the Residence of Yan, Duke of Zheng, we Write Poems on Bamboos (My Allotted Word for Rhyming is Fragrance)

New tips have just passed the wall,
From the green bamboos half-sheathed
   on the balance.
At night, their colors outshine book
   casings.
Over cups of wine, in coolness they can
   enhance.
Looking charming and clean in the rain,
They let winds blow forth their faint
   fragrance.
If only you stop your pruning,
Surely you will see them brush clouds in
   the long distance.

渝州候嚴六侍禦不到先下峽

聞道乘驄發，沙邊待至今。不知雲雨
散，虛費短長吟。山帶烏蠻闊，江連
白帝深。船經一柱觀，留眼共登臨。

At Yuzhou, I Waited for Censor Yan, the Sixth, in Vain, hence my Early Departure down the Gorges Alone

I heard you set out on a rare horse.
By the sands, until now I have been in
    wait.
In vain, I chant long and short poems,
Mindless of cloud and rain that dissipate.
Wide mountains reach the dark nomads.
To White Emperor City, on the deep
    river one can navigate.
As my boat passes One Pillar Temple,
I shall save it for our visit on another
    date.

陪李梓州王閬州蘇遂州李果州四使君登惠義寺

春日無人境，虛空不住天。鶯花隨世界，樓閣寄山巔。遲暮身何得，登臨意惘然。誰能解金印，瀟灑共安禪。

Climbing to Huiyi Temple, in the Company of Four Governors: Li of Zizhou, Wang of Langzhou, Su of Suizhou and Li of Guozhou

We seem to reach Nirvana with no
    abiding, in the void,
Climbing to a no-man's-land on a
    spring day.
Everywhere are orioles and flowers.
At the peak, towers and pavilions stay.
We have a mental block after ascending.
At an old age, from life what do we get
    for pay?
To meditate Buddha together in
    detachment,
Who among us can let our golden seals
    of office be taken away?

早發射洪縣南途中作

將老憂貧窶，筋力豈能及。征途乃侵星，得使諸病入。鄙人寡道氣，在困無獨立。詖裝逐徒旅，達曙淩險澀。寒日出霧遲，清江轉山急。僕夫行不進，駑馬若維縶。汀洲稍疏散，風景開怏悒。空慰所尚懷，終非曩遊集。衰顏偶一破，勝事難屢挹。茫然阮籍途，更灑楊朱泣。

Composed on my Way Southbound after Setting out Early from Shehong County

Getting old, I worry about poverty.
How can my strength stay?
I journey under stars.
Into my body, diseases make headway.

I lack the spirit of Daoism
And in hardship, fail to self-support as a
    mainstay.
With packed bags, I set out in a group,

33

Over dangerous spots, early in the day.

The sun breaks through the cold fog late.
A fast, limpid river winds around a hill.
My old horse looks as if tied up.
My servant moves on in vain.

Shoals spread out here and there.
The scenery dispels my sorrow.
This is a mere distraction of my present
    mood,
Not really like the places I used to go.

I may wear a smile on my worn face for
    once,
But often it is hard to have the same
    joyous imagination in play.
In confusion, I follow Ruan Ji, a recluse
    of yesterday
And weep like Yang Zhu, on the road of
    life, if astray.

正月三日歸溪上有作簡院內諸公

野外堂依竹。籬邊水向城。蟻浮仍臘
味，鷗泛已春聲。藥許鄰人剗，書從
稚子擎。白頭趨幕府，深覺負平生。

Composed on Returning to my Creek on the Third Day of the First Month, for the Gentlemen of the Official Compound

Waters by the hedge run towards the
city.
In the wilds, my cottage and bamboos
hang tight.
Despite foams like ants, my winter wine
keeps its flavor.
In spring, gulls are already calling in
flight.
My young child carries my books.
To my neighbor who wants to cut my
herbs, I grant the right.
When I run around at the headquarters,
with a head of white hair,
I deeply feel my betrayed life has lost

the fight.

通泉縣署壁後薛少保畫鶴

薛公十一鶴，皆寫青田真。畫色久欲盡，蒼然猶出塵。低昂各有意，磊落如長人。佳此志氣遠，豈惟粉墨新。萬里不以力，群遊森會神。威遲白鳳態，非是倉鶊鄰。高堂未傾覆，常得慰嘉賓。暴露牆壁外，終嗟風雨頻。赤霄有真骨，恥飲污池津。冥冥任所往，脫略誰能馴。

Cranes Painted by Xue Ji, Body Guard of the Prince, on a Mural at the Back of a Wall of the Tongquan County Office Building

The eleven painted cranes of Mister Xue
Are real portraits of those at Greenfield
   of a bygone year.
After a long time, the pigments are

almost gone.
They still belong to Fairyland, though
gray and bare.

The cranes look up or down, in different
moods,
Like tall people, with poise in view.
Splendid is their will to fly afar,
A spirit shown not just because the color
was new.

Effortlessly they cover myriad miles,
With a common spirit, flying en masse.
They may not match the grace of white
phoenixes,
But the likes of orioles are not their class.

Before the high hall collapsed,
The cranes pleased the honored guests.
Now left exposed on an outside wall,
Regrets over their eventual erosion by
wind and rain are expressed.

Some birds feel shamed to drink from
filthy ponds.

These are real birds from the red sky.
Who can tame those with free spirits?
They go where they want, far and high.

草堂即事

荒村建子月，獨樹老夫家。霧裏江船渡，風前徑竹斜。寒漁依密藻，宿鷺起圓沙。蜀酒禁愁得，無錢何為賒。

Current Events at my Thatched Cottage

By a lone tree is this old man's house,
In a deserted village, at the first month
    of the year.
A boat crosses the river in the fog.
By the front path, bamboos in the wind
    fail to stand upright.
Chilled fish stay close to dense algae.
Rising from whirled sands, egrets fly off
    to spend the night.
Shu wine can suppress my sorrow.

Penniless, where can I find brew to
spare?

朝雨

涼氣曉蕭蕭，江雲亂眼飄。風鴛藏近
渚，雨燕集深深。黃綺終辭漢，巢由
不見堯。草堂樽酒在，幸得過清朝。

Dawn Rain

The cool dawn air whistles again and
again.
Above the river, in a disarray floating
clouds have lain.
Wind-blown ducks hide near an islet.
Swallows gather amid deep branches in
the rain.
Huang and Qi, as hermits, did not serve
the Han king.
Refusing to see King Yao, Chaofu and
Xu You spurned any gain.
By luck, I get to pass the clear morn,

In my thatched cottage, where jugs of
   wine remain.

初冬

垂老戎衣窄，歸休寒色深。漁舟上急
水，獵火著高林。日有習池醉，愁來
梁甫吟。干戈未偃息，出處遂何心。

Early Winter

My army uniform feels tight as I get old.
Returning to rest, I sense how deep
   wintry colors can grow.
Hunting fires shine through tall forests.
Against swift currents, fishing boats go.

Daily I get well drunk
And chant the dirge "Liangfu" in sorrow.
Battles have not ceased.
Which career path, to my heart's content,
   should I follow?

陳拾遺故宅

拾遺平昔居，大屋尚修椽。悠揚荒山
日，慘淡故園煙。位下曷足傷，所貴
者聖賢。有才繼騷雅，哲匠不比肩。
公生楊馬後，名與日月懸。同遊英俊
人，多秉輔佐權。彥昭超玉價，郭振
起通泉。到今素壁滑，灑翰銀鉤連。
盛事會一時，此堂豈千年。終古立忠
義，感遇有遺篇。

The Former Residence of Reminder Chen Ziang

The former residence of the Reminder
Has the beams of the big house still
　　under repair.
Slowly sunlight passes over deserted
　　hills.
The misty old garden is worn and bare.

A low rank in the palace is no cause for
　　lament.
About sages and worthies he did care.

He was head and shoulders above all
   in any career.
With Li Sao and the Odes, his writings
   can well compare.

He had fame as high as the sun and the
   moon,
 Though unlike Yang Xiong and Sima
   Xiangru, born in a later year.
He befriended mostly the elite with
   power.
In politics, he dealt with issues entrusted
   him with care.

Zhao Yanzhao exceeded the worth of
   jade.
From a sheriff in Tongquan, Chancellor
   Zhao Yanzhen rose.
Even today on glossy white walls of this
   house,
Like silver hooks, on scrolls each
   calligraphic style shows.

Fabulous events happened just once.
For a thousand years, how can this

house survive?
He stood for loyalty and righteousness
for all time.
His poems "Moved by my Encounters"
let the ancient poetic style revive.

野望

金華山北涪水西，仲冬風日始淒淒。
山連越嶲蟠三蜀，水散巴渝下五溪。
獨鶴不知何事舞，飢烏似欲向人啼。
射洪春酒寒仍綠，目極傷神為誰攜。

Gazing at the Wilderness

North of Mount Jinhua and west of
River Fu,
It starts to be bleak in mid-winter, on a
windy day.
Waters spread over Ba and Yu as Five
Creeks.
Hills entwine Shu's Three Regions,
joining Yuexi Commadery in the lay.

A lone crane dances for a reason I do
　　not know.
There is cawing seemingly from a
　　starving crow.
Shehong County's spring wine is still
　　green in the cold.
I feel tired after straining my eyes, with
　　no wine coming my way.

進艇

南京久客耕南畝，北望傷神坐北窗。
畫引老妻乘小艇，晴看稚子浴清江。
俱飛蛺蝶無相逐，並蒂芙蓉本自雙。
茗飲蔗漿攜所有，瓷罌無謝玉為缸。

Getting on a Boat

Sitting by my north window, I look
　　northwards in sorrow,
As a southern farmer and a guest in the
　　south capital for a long stay.
I watch my young boy bathe in the sunlit,

limpid river,
And take my wife to sail in a small boat
by day.
Lotus blooms on a single stalk are
naturally paired.
Butterflies flying together do not chase
each other in disarray.
I have brought all I own to go with cane
syrup.
Jade crocks and porcelain jars are
treated in the same way.

晚秋陪嚴鄭公摩訶池泛舟
（得溪字）

湍駛風醒酒，船廻霧起堤。高城秋自
落，雜樹晚相迷。坐觸鴛鴦起，巢傾
翡翠低。莫須驚白鷺，為伴宿清溪。

In Late Autumn, Accompanying Yan, Duke of Zheng, Sailing on Moke Pond (With the Allotted Word "Brook")

On a fast turning boat, with rising fog
    from the bank,
In the wind, from the effects of wine I
    woke.
Autumn leaves fell by high city walls.
At mixed trees at night, we gave a
    lost look.
Kingfishers descended from their
    upturned nests.
When touched, to the air crouching
    mandarin ducks took.
There was no need to alarm white egrets,
That could overnight with us near a
    clear brook.

陪王侍禦同登東山最高頂宴姚通泉晚攜酒泛江

姚公美政誰與儔，不減昔時陳太丘。
邑中上客有柱史，多暇日陪驄馬遊。
東山高頂羅珍羞，下顧城郭銷我憂。
清江白日落欲盡，復攜美人登彩舟。
笛聲憤怒哀中流，妙舞逶迤夜未休。
燈前往往大魚出，聽曲低昂如有求。
三更風起寒波湧，取樂喧呼覺船重。
滿空星河光破碎，四座賓客色不動。
諸公臨深莫相違，迴船罷酒上馬歸。
人生歡會豈有極，無使霜過霑人衣。

In the Company of Attendant Censor Wang, we Climbed the Highest Peak of East Mount Where we were Feasted by Yao of Tongquan; in the Evening, we Took Wine and Went Boating on the River

In governance, who can match Lord
　　Yan's sound way?
He can compare well with Chen of

Taiqiu of yesterday.
Among honored guests in this town is
   one from the Censorate.
Much leisure lets him roam daily with
   his dappled gray.

At the peak of East Mount, tasty food is
   on display.
The view of the city wall clears my
   worries away.
Then we escort fair ladies onto a painted
   boat,
On a limpid stream, towards the end of
   the day.

With sadness, flute notes of anger and
   resentment we hear.
Wonderful dance steps in circles go on
   all night long.
Before lamps, often big fish appear,
Nodding as if begging as they listen to
   each song.

Cold waves surge as wind rises at
   midnight.

The boat seems heavy with our shouts in
    delight.
All the guests do not look concerned.
The broken Milky Way in the full sky is
    not bright.

My lords, under danger, please heed
    what is due.
Turn the boat and gallop home; the wine
    party is through.
In endless joys of life, we can get lost.
Do not let your robe get wet after a frost.

冬到金華山觀因得故拾遺陳公學堂遺跡

涪右眾山內，金華紫崔嵬。上有蔚藍
天，垂光抱瓊台。繫舟接絕壁，杖策
窮縈回。四顧俯層巔，淡然川谷開。
雪嶺日已死，霜鴻有餘哀。焚香玉女
跪，霧裏仙人來。陳公讀書堂，石柱
仄青苔。悲同為我起，激烈傷雄才。

In Winter, at a Daoist Temple on Mount Jinhua, I found the Relics of the Study Hall of Reminder Chen Ziang

Mount Jinhua is purplish, high and steep,
Among many by River Fu's right.
Above is the wide blue sky,
Embracing the jade terrace with sunlight.

I moored my boat by the cliff.
With my cane, I pushed ahead on a
    windy trail.
All around I could see tiered peaks
While streams and valleys looked pale.

Wild swans in the frost appeared over
    cheerless.
Of sunshine, snowy ridges were
    deprived.
Incense burned in a censor like a
    kneeling jade maiden.
In the fog, fairies arrived.

In the study hall of Lord Chen,

A stone column with green moss lay
  bent.
A mournful wind rose for me,
Over the loss of this great talent in
  lament.

去秋行

去秋涪江木落時，臂槍走馬誰家兒。
到今不知白骨處，部曲有去皆無歸。
遂州城中漢節在，遂州城外巴人稀。
戰場冤魂每夜哭，空令野營猛士悲。

Last Autumn: a Ballad

Who was that fellow, galloping with a
  lance in his hand,
As leaves dropped by River Fu last fall?
Even now, we know not where his white
  bones lie.
The troops that left did not return at all.
Within the walls of Suizhou, standards
  of Han remain.

Outside, few Ba people come in sight.

Brave soldiers sadden in the camps of
wilderness.

On the battlefield, souls of the wrongful
dead weep each night.

赴青城縣出成都寄陶王二少尹

老被樊籠役，貧嗟出入勞。客情投異
縣，詩態憶吾曹。東郭滄江合，西山
白雪高。文章差底病，回首興滔滔。

**Leaving Chengdu on my Way to
Qingcheng County, Sent to Two Vice-
Prefects: Tao and Wang**

Belabored and dislocated in the cage of
life,

This poor, old man sighs over his plight.

With a wanderer's mindset, I settle in a
strange county,

But recall how poets used to write.

The gray river unites by the east walls.

White snow on west hills reaches a
  height.
What disease can writings cure?
Looking back, I am flooded by
  inspiration in delight.

崔評事弟許相迎不到應慮老夫見泥雨
　　怯出必愆佳期走筆戲簡

江閣要賓許馬迎，午時起坐自天明。
浮雲不負青春色，細雨何孤白帝城。
身過花閒霑濕好，醉於馬上往來輕。
虛疑皓首衝泥怯，實少銀鞍傍險行。

My Cousin, Case Reviewer Cui, Offered to Escort me to his Place, but None Came. He should be thinking that an Old Man Like me Would Fear Going out at the Sight of Mud and Rain and Must Have Missed the Date. I Dashed this off as a Playful Note.

An important guest was offered a ride to
    your riverside pavilion.
In wait from dawn to noon, I have been
    sitting tight.
Drifting clouds do not darken fresh
    spring colors.
How can rain isolate White Emperor
    City when it is slight?
Moving past flowers, I think wetting
    the body is fine.
Drunk on horseback, I gallop back and
    forth, just feeling light.
It is really the lack of a silver saddle for
    my trip in danger,
Not your suspicion of a white-haired
    man dashing through mud in fright.

水檻遣心二首，其一

去郭軒楹敞，無村眺望賒。澄江平少岸，幽樹晚多花。細雨魚兒出，微風燕子斜。城中十萬戶，此地兩三家。

My Thoughts on a Floating Deck, no.1

Away from city walls, the deck with
    pillars,
Without villages around, lends an open
    view.
The limpid stream levels with a
    receding bank.
On secluded twigs, many late bloomers
    appear anew.
Fish emerge in the fine rain.
Aslant in the breeze, swallows fly
    through.
Compared to the ten thousand
    households in the city,
Families here are few.

水檻遣心二首，其二

蜀天常夜雨，江檻已朝晴。葉潤林塘
密，衣乾枕席清。不堪祗老病，何得
尚浮名。淺把涓涓酒，深憑送此生。

My Thoughts on a Floating Deck, no. 2

The dawn sun is already on my deck and
the river.
In Shu, rain always falls from the night
sky.
Dense, moist leaves are in ponds and
forests.
My pillow and mat look clean; my robes
stay dry.
I cannot bear just being old and sick.
How come my fame is still fatuous after
I try?
Let me taste my wine in trickles,
To really while away my days until I die

君不見簡蘇徯

君不見道邊廢棄池，君不見前者摧折
桐。百年死樹中琴瑟，一斛舊水藏蛟
龍。丈夫蓋棺事始定，君今幸未成老
翁，何恨憔悴在山中。深山窮谷不可
處，霹靂魍魎兼狂風。

A Note for Su Xi
(Have you not Seen)

Have you not seen
An abandoned pond by the pathway?
Have you not seen
Before us, a snapped firmiana in decay?
A dead tree after a hundred years can be
　　a lute or harp.
A measure of stagnant water hides a
　　flood dragon.
Only after closing a coffin can we
　　judge a person.
You have not become an old man today.
What lament wears you down in the
　　hills?

With thunders, goblins and gusts,
From remote hilly ravines, stay away.

贈蘇四徯

異縣昔同遊，各云厭轉蓬。別離已五
年，尚在行李中。戎馬日衰息，乘輿
安九重。有才何棲棲，將老逮所窮。
為郎未為賤，其奈疾病攻。子何鸒
黑，不得豁心胸。巴蜀倦剽劫，下愚
成土風。幽薊已削平，荒徼尚彎弓。
斯人脫身來，豈非吾道東。乾坤雖寬
大，所適裝囊空。肉食哂菜色，少壯
欺老翁。況乃主客閒，古來偪側同。
君今下荊揚，獨帆如飛鴻。二州豪俠
場，人馬皆自雄。一請甘飢寒，再請
甘養蒙。

Presented to Su Xi, the Fourth

We once roamed together in another

county.
About our weariness of resembling
    tumbleweeds, we say.
Five years have passed since we parted.
We are still wandering today.

War-horses weaken and retire each day.
Behind nine gates, the imperial coach is
    secure.
You are talented, so why do you worry?
With resignation, I accept being old
    and poor as my failure.

Being a member of the palace staff is
    not low in status.
I cannot fight my disease.
Why do you look so tanned?
Your mind is ill at ease.

You are tired of the pillage in Ba and
    Shu.
Local customs are stupid and base.
Peace in You and Ji has been restored.
Frontier wastelands are still in a combat
    phase.

On your way east, this poem will keep
    you company.
I escaped war to come here.
Through the universe is vast,
My luggage is empty wherever I appear.

Meat eaters sneer at how vegetarians
    look.
On and on, harassment of old people by
    the young goes.
Moreover, between natives and aliens,
Uneasiness rises when they are too close.

Sir, you are now going downstream to
    Jing and Yang,
With a lone sail, like a wild swan in
    flight.
In these two prefectures, knights-errant
    gather.
Both men and horses show fight.

First, I pray that you accept being cold
    and hungry.
Second, I pray that you nurture your

mind from any mental blight.

奉酬嚴公寄題野亭之作

拾遺曾奏數行書，懶性從來水竹居。
奉引濫騎沙苑馬，幽棲真釣錦江魚。
謝安不倦登臨費，阮籍焉知禮法疏。
枉沐旌麾出城府，草茅無徑欲教鋤。

Respectfully in Answer to the Poem of
Lord Yan: "On my Wilderness Pavilion"

My writings as a reminder once came
   through to the king.
Being idle, I have always lived by water
   and bamboo.
I angle hard for fish in the Brocade
   River in seclusion.
The honor to let me ride a horse from
   the royal stable is undue.
Xie An did not get tired of paying for
   mountain climbing.

About his rudeness, Ruan Ji never knew.
Your visit with banners and guards from
   the city is not impromptu.
Before my thatched cottage, I shall have
   the path cleaned for you.

奉贈射洪李四丈

丈人屋上烏，人好烏亦好。人生意氣
豁，不在相逢早。南京亂初定，所向
色枯槁。遊子無根株，茅齋付秋草。
東征下月峽，掛席窮海島。萬里須十
金，妻孥未相保。蒼茫風塵際，蹭蹬
麒麟老。志士懷感傷，心胸已傾倒。

Respectfully Presented to Sir Li, the Fourth, of Shehong County

Sir, at your rooftop is a crow.
If you are kind, we love your crow also.
The openness and generosity you show
Depend not on friendship formed years

ago.

After the turmoil of the south capital,
People look worn wherever I go.
Like fall grass, my thatched cottage
     fades,
I am a rootless, wandering fellow.

I shall set sail to all islands of the sea.
My eastern trip will lead me to Bright
     Moon Gorge below.
I need ten weights of gold to travel afar.
The protection of my wife and children,
     I forego.

Amid mud and dust, in the hazy void,
Old and weak, a unicorn can grow.
I am overwhelmed with admiration
Over your high aims, pained concern
     and credo.

奉送崔都水翁下峽

無數涪江筏，鳴橈總發時。別離終不
久，宗族忍相遺。白狗黃牛峽，朝雲
暮雨祠。所過憑問訊，到日自題詩。

Respectfully Seeing off Mister Cui of the Department of the Waterways down the Gorges

In setting out together, the oars resound
    on River Fu,
From countless rafts in a chain.
Our parting will come soon.
Leaving a relative causes unbearable
    pain.
The gorges have names: White Dog and
    Yellow Ox.
You will see the shrine with dawn
    clouds and evening rain.
Wherever you pass, I trust you to send
    my regards.
I shall write poems when I get there
    again.

奉觀嚴鄭公廳事岷山沱江畫圖十韻

沱水臨中座，岷山到北堂。白波吹粉
壁，青嶂插彫梁。直訝杉松冷，兼疑
菱荇香。雪雲虛點綴，莎草得微茫。
嶺雁隨毫末，川蜺飲練光。霏紅洲蕊
亂，拂黛石蘿長。暗谷非關雨，丹楓
不為霜。秋成玄圃外，景物洞庭旁。
繪事功殊絕，幽襟與激昂。從來謝太
傅，丘壑道難忘。

Seeing a Painting of Mount Min and River Tuo, in the Courtroom of Yan Wu, Duke of Zheng, in Ten Couplets

River Tuo makes its presence before the
  seats.
Mount Min reaches North Hall, it seems.
On the plaster walls are blown white
  waves.
Green cliffs pierce carved beams.

I suspect water caltrops and floating
  hearts emit fragrance,

First awed by the look of fir and pine in
   the cold.
With a hint of cloud and snow,
The blurry and minimal treatment of
   sedges is not bold.

From the painter's brush come wild
   geese above peaks
And drinking from a stream, a bright,
   silken waterfall.
On an isle, red petals shower like a riot.
Brushing against a black rock, long
   creepers fall.

I find dark valleys and red maples,
But the background does not include
   frost or rain.
It is a late fall scene, beyond Xuanpu for
   immortals,
Reminding me of the landscape by Lake
   Dongting again.

The art of the painter is special and rare,
With the passion of a recluse at heart.
Grand Tutor Xie An served the king.

With the hermit's hill and ravine, he
found it hard to part.

送梓州李使君之任

籍甚黃丞相，能名自穎川。近看除刺
史，還喜得吾賢。五馬何時到，雙魚
會早傳。老思筇柱杖，冬要錦衾眠。
不作臨歧恨，惟聽舉最先。火雲揮汗
日，山鐸醒心泉。遇害陳公殞，于今
蜀道憐。君行射洪縣，為我一潸然。

Seeing off Commissioner Li of Zizhou Coming to Take up his Post

You are another Prime Minister Huang
of Han
Who got his fame in Ying Chuan, under
his rein.
Of late, your work as a prefect.
Gladdens us for a wise man we obtain.

When will your five-horse entourage
    bring you to your post?
I hope for your letters by paired carps
    without delay.
I want a brocade quilt to sleep in winter
And, being old, think of a Qiong
    bamboo cane.

Let me hear your priority in promoting
    excellence.
And end my regret of your being away.
The sun with fiery clouds makes you
    wipe your sweat.
A spring keeps you alert at a station by
    a mountain.

Even today, those on the roads of Shu
    pity Mister Chen,
A gentleman who died in harm's way.
As you pass through Shehong County,
For my sake, please shed streaming
    tears of pain.

送段公曹歸廣州

南海春天外，公曹幾月程。峽雲籠樹
小，湖日落船明。交趾丹砂重，韶州
白葛輕。幸君因旅客，時寄錦官城。

Seeing off Duan of the Personnel Evaluation Section on his Return to Guangzhou

To reach the South Sea beyond the
spring sky,
How many months does it take you to
your work site?
In the gorge, trees covered by clouds
appear small.
The sunlit ship on the lake looks bright.
Cinnabar pellets of Jiaozhi are heavy.
The white linen of Shaozhou is light.
I would feel lucky if a traveler should
send something,
To Brocade City when the timing is
right.

寄杜位

近聞寬法離新州，想見懷歸尚百憂。
逐客雖皆萬里去，悲君已是十年流。
干戈況復塵隨眼，鬢髮還應雪滿頭。
玉壘題書心緒亂，何時更得曲江遊。

Sent to Du Wei

You left Xinzhou due to lax rules, I
heard of late.
I can imagine how your much worried
mind would relate.
Although all banished must leave for
endless miles away.
My sadness is over your release after
ten years in wait.
Besides the dust of war that follows
your eyes,
Your hair should be snow white, at any
rate.
By Yulei Hill, I write you a letter, ill at
ease.
For our trip at Qujiang Waterway, when
is the date?

范二員外邀吳十侍禦鬱特枉駕闕展待聊寄此

暫往比鄰去，空聞二妙歸。幽棲誠簡略，衰白已光輝。野外貧家遠，村中好客稀。論文或不愧，肯重款柴扉。

Supernumerary Fan Miao, the Second and Vice Censor Wu Yu, the Tenth, Came for a Special Visit, but I was not Present to Receive them, so I Send this

I have been to my neighbor's briefly
And heard of fine visitors in a pair.
Your visit brightens the home of a worn,
    white-haired man.
My hut in seclusion is really bare.
This poor house lies far in the wilds.
Friendly visitors to this village are rare.
Would you favor me with a re-visit at
    my ramshackle gate?
In discussing literature, I may feel no
    shame to share.

71

魏十四侍禦就弊廬相別

有客騎驄馬，江邊問草堂，遠尋留藥
價，惜別到文場。入幕旌旗動，歸軒
錦繡香。時應念衰疾，書疏及滄浪。

Vice Censor-in-chief, the Fourteenth, Comes to my Humble Hut to Say Goodbye

To my thatched cottage by the river,
A visitor came on a dappled gray.
Seeking me from afar, he paid for my
    herbs,
Stopping by a writer's place before
    going away.
Entering the headquarters, with banners
    waving,
He will return to a study with scented
    brocade to stay.
From time to time, he should think of
    my illness
And write me in seclusion some day.

徐九少伊見過

晚景孤村僻，行軍數騎來。交新徒有
喜，禮厚愧無才。賞靜憐雲竹，忘歸
步月台。何當看花蕊，欲發照江梅。

Vice Governor Xu, the Ninth, Stopped by

You came with several outriders
To my remote, lone village at twilight.
My lack of talent matches not your high
    courtesy
Though, with shame, I got to greet a
    new friend with delight.
You forgot to return, pacing my moonlit
    terrace
And appreciated quietude, with lovely
    bamboos at the clouds' height.
When will you come again for flowers?
Riverside plum trees about to bloom
    shine bright.

觀薛稷少保書畫壁

少保有古風，得之陝郊篇。惜哉功名
忤，但見書畫傳。我遊梓州東，遺跡
涪江邊。畫藏青蓮界，書入金榜懸。
仰看垂露姿，不崩亦不騫。鬱鬱三大
字，蛟龍岌相纏。又揮西方變，發地
扶木掀。慘澹壁飛動，到今色未填。
此行疊壯觀，郭薛俱才賢。不知百載
後，誰復來通泉。

Viewing the Calligraphy and Mural
by Xue Ji, Body Guard of the Prince

The body guard wrote in the "Classic
    Style".
From his poem "Shan Outskirts", this
    view we gain.
Regrettably, his rank and honor suffered,
But his calligraphy and painting remain.

In my travel east of Zizhou,
Beside River Fu, for his relics kept,
I find his calligraphy hung on a plaque

in gold,
And in a Buddhist temple, his painting
    upkept.

I raise my eyes for his calligraphy in
    "Hanging Dew" style,
With a composition, balanced and well-
    defined.
Three huge characters look full-bodied
    and supple,
Like flood dragons perilously entwined.

His brush produces Buddhist
    transformation images from the west.
From the ground up, the mural is held
    by studs all the way.
The wall seems to be flying in the dark.
No color has been added even today.

Guo and Xue are talented worthies.
On this trip, two grand views I obtain.
I know not a hundred years from now,
To Tongquan, if anyone will come again.

野望

納納乾坤大，行行郡國遙。雲山兼五嶺，風壤帶三苗。野樹侵江潤，春浦長雪消。扁舟空老去，無補聖明朝。

Views of the Wilds

Between the big, encompassing Heaven
    and Earth,
I travel afar on a strange terrain.
Cloudy hills link with Five Mountains.
Land and customs form the Three
    Miaos' domain.
Nameless trees dominate this wide
    riverscape.
Spring reeds grow as long-term
    snowfalls wane.
In a small boat, I age in vain,
Giving no help to our saintly, glorious
    reign.

嚴中丞枉駕見過

元戎小隊出郊坰，問柳尋花到野亭。
川合東西瞻使節，地分南北任流萍。
扁舟不獨如張翰，皂帽還應似管寧。
寂寞江天雲霧裏，何人道有少微星。

The Visit by Vice Censor-in-chief Yan Wu

The commander and a few guards come
   to the outskirts,
Reaching my wild cottage, past many a
   flower and willow.
You command the east and west circuits
   of Sichuan.
South or north, like duckweeds, I drift
   with the flow.
Unlike Zhang Han, in my small boat I
   meet no benefactor.
With a hermit's black cap, I resemble
   Guan Ning long ago.
Who talked about a constellation for
   recluses?
The sky and river are quiet and misty,

above and below.

客至

舍南舍北皆春水，但見群鷗日日來。
花徑不曾緣客掃，蓬門今始為君開。
盤餐市遠無兼味，樽酒家貧只舊醅。
肯與鄰翁相對飲，隔籬呼取盡餘杯。

Visitor coming

South and north of my hut runs spring
    waters.
Every day I see flocks of gulls come
    through.
The path with flowers have not been
    swept.
The bramble gate is now open for you.
Far from the market, my dishes are few.
I am poor; my ale is not new.
The man next door may care to join me.
I shall shout over the hedge so we finish
    off the brew.

過客相尋

窮老真無事，江山已定居。地幽忘盥
櫛，客至罷琴書。掛壁移筐果，呼兒
問煮魚。時聞繫舟楫，及此問吾廬。

Visitors Come by Looking for Me

Nothing really happens to a poor, old
    man.
By this hill and river, I have already
    settled to stay.
In seclusion, I forget to wash and comb.
When guests come, I put my zither and
    books away.
Baskets of fruits on walls are removed.
To boil fish, I ask my son for the way.
Visitors on arrival ask about my cottage,
Having moored, any time, any day.

王竟攜酒高亦同過共用寒字

臥疾荒郊遠，通行小徑難。故人能領
客，攜酒重相看。自愧無鮭菜，空煩
卸馬鞍。移樽勸山簡，頭白恐風寒。

Wang Brought Wine and Gao Came too for a Visit (We all Used the Word 'Cold' to Rhyme)

I lie sick afar in the deserted wilds.
A small through path is hard to unfold.
Your revisit comes with wine and
    another guest,
From a friend since the days of old.
I have troubled you to unsaddle your
    horses,
Shamed over the peasant food in my
    household.
I ply my guests, heavy drinkers like
    Shan Jian, with ale.
A white-haired head is prone to catch a
    cold.

哭韋大夫之晉

I

淒愴郇瑕邑，差池弱冠年。丈人叨禮
數，文律早周旋。臺閣黃圖裏，簪裾
紫蓋邊。尊榮真不忝，端雅獨脩然。
貢喜音容閒，馮招病疾纏。南過駭倉
卒，北思悄聯綿。鵩鳥長沙諱，犀牛
蜀郡憐。素車猶慟哭，寶劍欲高懸。
漢道中興盛，韋經亞相傳。沖融標世
業，磊落映時賢。

II

城府深朱夏，江湖眇霽天。綺樓關樹
頂，飛旐泛堂前。帟幕欹風燕，笳簫
急暮蟬。興殘虛白室，跡斷孝廉船。
童孺交遊盡，喧卑俗事牽。老來多涕
淚，情在強詩篇。誰繼方隅理，朝難
將帥權。春秋褒貶例，名器重雙全。

81

Weeping for Grand Master Wei Zhijun

I

Dreary and sad is the town of Xunxia.
We were almost twenty in a yesteryear.
Your honor favored me with your
   company.
We early on discussed rules of writing
   in a pair.

You served in ministries in Changan
And as a prefect by Mount Heng, in
   your office dress.
Truly you deserve prestige and honor.
Poise and grace guide how you express.

Gong Yu liked your professional
   manners.
A patron like Feng Tang may summon
   me, but I am ill.
Coming south, I was shocked by your
   sudden death.
My yearnings for the north are not still.

The owl is a bad omen in Changsha.
Stone rhinos are symbols that Shu
    people love to accept.
By the funeral carriage, all wept bitterly.
Like the sword hung high at a grave, my
    promises to you will be kept.

The Han culture has flourished after
    restoration.
Like Wei Xian, you promoted the
    classics and your son will follow.
Open-minded and cheerful, you leave a
    lofty legacy.
Free and easy, with current worthies you
    can keep your fame aglow.

II

City buildings stand in red hot summer.
Over river and lake, the chance of a
    clear sky is small.
Grand mansions overshoot treetops
Many flags flap before the hall.

Drapes in the wind slow down swallows.
Shrill notes of flutes, reed pipes and
   evening cicadas I hear.
My uninspired mind draws a blank.
My benefactor will never appear.

Gone are my childhood friends.
I feel held back by everyday matters,
   rowdy and trite.
Getting old, I often shed tears.
I force myself to compose verses when
   my mood is right.

Who will continue to mind the frontiers?
The court cannot easily grant the
   general's authority to anyone.
In the rule to appraise historical figures,
Both reputation and morals should be
   used, not just one.

王十七侍禦掄許攜酒至草堂奉寄此詩便請邀高三十五使君同到

老夫臥穩朝慵起，白屋寒多暖始開。
江鸛巧當幽徑浴，鄰雞還過短牆來。
皂蓋能忘折野梅，戲假霜威促山簡。
須成一醉習池迴，繡衣屢許攜家醞。

With Wine, Attendant Censor Wang Lun, the Seventeenth, Promises to Come to my Thatched Cottage; Respectfully I Send this Poem and Invite him to Visit along with Governor Gao, the Thirty-fifth

My cold, worn house has begun to get warm.
I lie snugly, too lazy to rise at the break of day.
A neighbor's chickens again cross over the low wall.
River storks bathe right by a secluded pathway.
Wang, in an embroidered robe, often

85

brings his house wine.
Will Gao with his black hat forget to
cut wild plum flowers in a spray?
For fun, let me frostily order my guests
before returning,
Like Shan Jian at Xi Pool, to be drunk
all the way.

立秋後題

日月不相饒，節序昨夜隔。玄蟬無停
號，秋燕已如客。平生獨往願，惆悵
年半百。罷官亦由人，何事拘形役。

Written after the Beginning of Autumn

Days and months show us no leniency.
Last night, a seasonal change was
addressed.
Black cicadas do not stop their calls.
Each swallow in fall is already a
departing guest.

For my whole life, I wish to set out
    alone.
That my age is fifty leaves me depressed.
Resignation from office starts with the
    individual.
To labor my mind and body, why am I
    so hard pressed?

嚴鄭公階下新松（得霑字）

弱質豈自負，移根方爾瞻。細聲聞玉
帳。疏翠近珠簾，未見紫煙集，虛蒙
清露霑。何當一百丈，欹蓋擁高簷。

The Young Pine below the Stairs of Yan, Duke of Zheng, with the Allotted Word "Wet" for Rhyming

After being transplanted, you are now
    noticed.
To be self-supporting, how does your
    weak body get?
Your light green form nears the pearl

curtain.
Across the jade tent, let me hear your
  murmur yet.
There is no purple mist on you,
Just some clear dew making you wet.
When will you be a hundred yards tall,
Hugging high eaves, aslant as a coverlet?

Year 765-767

茅堂檢校收稻二首，其一

香稻三秋末，平田百傾閒。喜無多屋
宇，幸不礙雲山。禦裌侵寒氣，嘗新
破旅顏。紅鮮終日有，玉粒未吾慳。

At my Thatched Hall, Overseeing a Harvest of Rice, no 1

From level fields of about a hundred
  acres,
By late fall, a harvest of fragrant rice is
  due.

Glad to see few houses around,
I feel lucky to have no clouds on hills
   to block the view.
Cold air seeps past my lined robe.
A wanderer smiles on tasting something
   new.
I do not hold back eating jade-like rice,
Red and fresh, available all day through.

茅堂檢校收稻二首，其二

稻米炊能白，秋葵煮復新。誰云滑易
飽，老藉軟俱勻。種幸房州熟，苗同
伊闕春。無勞映渠碗，自有色如銀。

At my Thatched Hall, Overseeing a Harvest of Rice, no 2

Boiled mallows take on a new look.
Cooked rice can appear white.
Who says smooth mallows fill one up
   easily?
Soft rice helps old people sustain.

My harvest from seeds called
  "Fangzhou Ripe"
Has sprouts like "Yique Spring" in
  strain.
Do not bother to heap them in big bowls
  to show the sheen.
The silver color naturally comes in sight.

季秋蘇五弟纓江樓夜宴崔十三評事韋
少府姪三首，其一

峽險江驚急，樓高月迴明。一時今夕
會，萬里故鄉情。星落黃姑渚，秋辭
白帝城。老人因酒病，堅坐看君傾。

**At the End of Autumn, my Younger
Cousin Su Ying, the Fifth, Holds a
Feast for my Nephews: Criminal
Judge Cui, the Thirteenth and Sheriff
Wei, at his Riverside Tower, no.1**

By steep gorges and fast fearful waves,
This high tower is moonlit bright.

We are homesick endless miles away,
In a gathering tonight.
It is past autumn in White Emperor City.
The constellation "Yellow Maiden
    Sandbar" has no starlight.
Sick from too much wine,
I just watch people drink and sit tight.

季秋蘇五弟纓江樓夜宴崔十三評事韋
少府姪三首，其二

對月那無酒，登樓況有江。聽歌驚白
鬢，笑舞拓秋窗。尊蟻添相續，沙鷗
並一雙。盡憐君醉倒，更覺片心降。

**At the End of Autumn, my Younger
Cousin Su Ying, the Fifth, Holds a
Feast for my Nephews: Criminal
Judge Cui, the Thirteenth and Sheriff
Wei, at his Riverside Tower, no.2**

How can one lack wine facing the moon?
Besides, at an upper floor, a river shows.

Songs alarm this man with white hair.
In fall, our laughs and gestures push
   open windows.
Two sand gulls stay together.
Refilling of cups with lees follows.
I fully love seeing all get drunk.
Moreover, more relaxed my heart goes.

季秋蘇五弟纓江樓夜宴崔十三評事韋
少府姪三首，其三

明月生長好，浮雲薄漸遮。悠悠照邊
塞，悄悄憶京華。清動杯中物，高隨
海上查。不眠瞻白兔，百過落烏紗。

**At the End of Autumn, my Younger
Cousin Su Ying, the Fifth, Holds a
Feast for my Nephews: Criminal
Judge Cui, the Thirteenth and Sheriff
Wei, at his Riverside Tower, no.3**

Thin clouds move slowly over the moon
Which, after rising, looks fine.

Quietly I recall the capital.
On and on, frontier moonbeams shine.
It follows rafts at sea from a height
And shoots clearly into my cup of wine.
It often appears in a party of top poets.
To see White Hare in the moon, any
    sleep I decline.

江上值水如海勢聊短述

爲人性僻耽佳句，語不驚人死不休。
老去詩篇渾漫與，春來花鳥莫深愁。
新添水檻供垂釣，故著浮槎替入舟。
焉得思如陶謝手，今渠述作與同遊。

A Casual, Short Poem on the Occasion of Seeing a River Resembling a Sea

Naturally idiosyncratic, I indulge in
    well-written lines.
Until death, I shock people with the
    language I follow.

Old, I pretty much write casual verses.
Spring birds and flowers cause me no
   deep sorrow.
My new floating deck with railing for
   fishing
Replaces the need to take a boat to row.
How can I get to roam and write poems
With masters like Tao Qian and Xie An
   years ago?

偶題

I

文章千古事，得失寸心知。作者皆殊
列，名聲豈浪垂。騷人嗟不見，漢道
盛於斯。前輩飛騰入，餘波綺麗為。
後賢兼舊制，歷代各清規。法自儒家
有，心從弱歲疲。永懷江左逸，多病
鄴中奇。騄驥皆良馬，麒麟帶好兒。
車輪徒已斲，堂構惜仍虧。漫得潛夫
論，虛傳幼婦碑。

緣情慰飄蕩，抱疾屢遷移。經濟慚長
策，飛棲假一枝。塵沙傍蜂蠆，江峽
繞蛟螭。蕭瑟唐虞遠，聯翩楚漢危。
聖朝兼盜賊，異俗更喧卑。鬱鬱星辰
劍，蒼蒼雲雨池。兩都開幕府，萬宇
插軍麾。南海殘銅柱，東風避月支。
音書恨烏鵲，號怒怪熊羆。稼穡分詩
興，柴荊學工宜。故山迷白閣，秋水
憶黃陂。不敢要佳句，愁來賦別離。

A Chance Composition

I

Literature is passed down through the
 ages.
Merits and faults are truly known to the
 heart.
Writers of all genres are listed.
Fame is not casually given for their art.

I sigh for the absence of bards in the
    style of 'Li Sao'
From which Fu poetry of Han flourished
    after the beginning date.
Our predecessors wrote with vigor as if
    in flight,
Followed by a style considered ornate.

Still later, seasoned writers also made
    classical poetry,
Offering clean-cut rules for generations
    to uphold.
My philosophy follows Confucian
    teachings
Though my mental faculty suffers as I
    get old.

I often resent the strange customs of Ye
And forever recall people in South of
    the River, without a care.
Like Lu Ji, the fine horse, the Seven
    Masters of Jianan excelled.
Good colts come from steeds that are
    rare.

A wheelwright cannot make his son
    learn his trade.
Any reform to our society, like a worn
    hall, is of no avail.
Wang Fu wrote as a recluse, but my
    output is poor.
Handan Chun penned a piece for a girl's
    commemorative stele, but I fail.

II

Writing poetry from my heart consoles
    this wanderer
As I often move about, sick and
    distressed.
Ashamed for the lack of long-term
    planning for my finances,
In my flight, on a spot now I rest.

Flood dragons coil in rivers and gorges.
I stay by bees and scorpions, amid dust
    and sand.
Good kings in history are far from us in
    the cold.
Local and national unrests endanger our
    land.

Our holy dynasty and brigands coexist.
Rebels bring strange customs and loud
　　rowdiness.
Like the Seven Star Sword, forged near
　　green ponds, under cloud and rain,
In our culture, integrity is the value we
　　stress.

Military headquarters have been set up
　　in both capitals,
With army flags on countless posts.
Two brazen pillars remain to mark our
　　southern borders.
In the east wind, from Tibetans our king
　　fled for safe outposts.

I blame bears for their howling rage
And hate magpies for good news still
　　out of sight.
Farming robs me of time and inspiration
　　for poetry.
To deal with bramble and firewood, I
　　learn to do what is right.

Autumn waters remind me of
 Huang Pool.
To my hometown's White Pavilion
 uphill, my charmed memories go.
I dare not insist on producing fine lines
 of poetry,
Just writing on separation in sorrow.

上後園山腳

朱夏熱所嬰，清旭步北林。小園背高
岡，挽葛上崎崟。曠望延駐目，飄颻
散疏襟。潛鱗恨水壯，去翼依雲深。
勿謂地無疆，劣如山有陰。石楄遍天
下，水陸兼浮沉。自我登隴首，十年
經碧岑。劍門來巫峽，薄倚浩至今。
故園暗戎馬，骨肉失追尋。時危無消
息，老去多歸心。志士惜白日，久客
籍黃金。敢為蘇門嘯，庶作梁父吟。

Climbing the Foothills by my Rear Garden

Out of shape in torrid summer, I walk
In the north woods, in cool dawn light.
My small garden backs to a high ridge.
Grabbing kudzu vines, I climb steep
    slopes to a height.

A broad view draws my attentive eyes.
A breeze loosens my lapels and the tie.
Fish at the bottom hate strong currents.
Deep into clouds, departing birds fly.

Do not say the earth is boundless.
The shaded north hillside makes inferior
    farmland.
Shi Yuan trees are all over the world.
Living things may sink or float, in water
    or on land.

Ever since I take up farming,
For ten years, I pass tall green hills on
    my way.
From Sword Gate to Wu Gorge,

With thin resources, I got restless until
today.

With my hometown gloomy in war
And my own flesh and blood not found,
I get no news, in times of peril.
Aging, I mostly want to be homeward
bound.

A man of lofty goals treasures daylight.
A detained wanderer relies on gold.
Dare I do transcendental whistling, like
a recluse poet at Mount Sumen?
Making a dirge like "Song of Liangfu"
is the hope I hold.

曉望

白帝更聲盡，陽臺曙色分。高峰寒上
日，疊嶺宿霾雲。地坼江帆隱，天清
木葉聞。荊扉對麋鹿，應共爾為群。

Dawn View

Night-watch rattles stop at White
　　Emperor City.
Like those at Sun Terrace, dawn colors
　　look clear.
In the sunrise over cold, tall ridges,
Mist and clouds on layered peaks appear.
The ground splits; sails on the river get
　　hidden.
From a clear sky, the sounds of leaves I
　　hear.
I should be flocking, at my brushwood
　　gate,
With some nearby herds of deer.

廣州段功曹到，得楊五長史譚書。功
　　農卻歸，聊寄此詩

衛青開幕府，楊僕將樓船。漢節梅花
外，春城海水邊。銅梁書遠及，珠浦
使將旋。貧病地鄉老，煩君萬里傳。

Duan of the Personnel Evaluation Section Arrives from Guangzhou and Gives me a Letter from Military Officer Tan, the Fifth. Duan is Going back and I Send this Poem with him

Like Wai Qing, you set up your
    headquarters.
Yang commands his towered ship like
    Yang Pu before.
Han standards stay beyond plum blooms.
In spring, you have arrived from a city
    by the sea.
Afar from Tongliang, his letter came.
The bearer will return to Pearl River's
    shore.
Poor and sick, I age in a strange village.
May I trouble you to direct this poem for
    me?

八陣圖

功蓋三分國，名成八陣圖。江流石不
轉，遺恨失吞吳。

The Eight-part Battle Formation

In the tripartite states, Zhuge Liang got
   top fame.
His eight-part battle formation earned
   him a name.
The river flows on; the stone formation
   does not move.
Regrettably, on Wu he failed to take a
   claim.

南極

南極青山眾，西江白谷分。古城疏落
木，荒戍密寒雲。歲月蛇常見，風飆
虎或聞。近身皆鳥道，殊俗自人群。

睥睨登哀柝，蠻弧照夕曛。亂離多醉
尉，愁殺李將軍。

The Furthest South

West of the river, White Valley stands
  apart.
In this furthest south prefecture, many
  linked green hills show.
Dense cold clouds cover a deserted
  fortress.
Sparse trees in this old city grow.
Time passes; snakes are often seen.
Tigers are at times heard as gusts blow.
All nearby paths are birding trails.
Special customs are for locals to follow.
From watch-towers come cheerless
  beats of clappers.
At sunset, rebels' bow and arrow are
  aglow.
In turmoil, many drunk soldiers
Put able chiefs, like General Li, in dire
  sorrow.

宴王使君宅題二首，其一

漢王追韓信，蒼生起謝安。吾徒自漂
泊，世事各艱難。逆旅招邀近，他鄉
思緒寬。不才甘朽質，高臥豈泥蟠。

Feasting at Prefect Wang's House, no.1

Like Han Xin, you are eagerly sought
    by the king.
Like Xie An, you serve to lift people
    from their sad plight.
World events bring hardships to each.
In vain, I wander from site to site.
Your invitation at a nearby residence
Makes me, in a strange land, feel less
    uptight.
Untalented, I accept my worn condition,
Unlike a dragon coiled in mud that can
    later show fight.

宴王使君宅題二首， 其二

泛愛容霜髮，留歡上夜關。自吟詩送
老，相勸酒開顏。戎馬今何地，鄉園
獨舊山。江湖墮清月，酩酊任扶還。

Feasting at Prefect Wang's House, no.2

Your magnanimity takes in this man
    with white hair
And delays guests for joy with a shut
    gate at night.
I chant poems alone as I get old.
Your plying me with wine brings delight.
Right now, war horses are everywhere.
My hillside hometown is deserted at its
    former site.
Drunk, I let someone help me back.
All over, clear moonbeams shine bright.

宴戎州楊使君東樓

勝絕驚老身，情忘發興奇。座從歌伎
密，樂任主人為。重碧拈春酒，輕紅
掰荔枝。樓高欲愁思，橫笛未休吹。

Feasting at the Eastern Tower of Yang, Prefect of Rongzhou

The peerless view stuns this old man,
With my mood aroused and reserve shed,
Female singers crowd where we sit.
We have joys as the host would say.
The spring wine is in deep green.
We split open lichees in light red.
At a high tower, I am about to feel sad.
On horizontal flutes, they endlessly play.

宴忠州使君侄宅

出守吾家侄，殊方此日歡。自須游阮
舍，不是怕湖灘。樂助長歌逸，杯饒
旅思寬。昔曾如意舞，牽率強為看。

Feasting at the Residence of my Nephew, Prefect of Zhongzhou

As prefect, my nephew holds a feast
And in a strange place, entertains me on
    this day.
I fear not the lake rapids downstream,
But must visit the historical home of
    Ruan Ji of yesterday.
Cups of wine soothe the runaway mind
    of a drifter.
Music accompanying long songs helps
    us get carried away.
In the past, I danced with a ruyi staff.
I shall be an onlooker, if forced today.

社日兩篇，其一

九農成德業，百祀發光輝。報效神如
在，馨香舊不違。南翁巴曲醉，北雁
塞聲微。尚想東方朔，詼諧割肉歸。

Festival Days, no.1

Many farmers build ethical businesses.
A hundred rites shed light.
As in the old days, their fragrance stays.
The rewards, as if a godsend, make
    things right.
Old southerners get drunk in Ba music.
The sound of north wild geese at the
    frontiers is slight.
I think of Dongfeng Shuo who cut meat
    for himself in the palace.
Of the misconduct before the king, he
    wittily made light.

社日兩篇，其二

陳平亦分肉，太史竟論功。今日江南
老，他時渭北童。歡娛看絕塞，涕淚
落秋風。鴛鷺迴金闕，誰憐病峽中。

Festival Days, no.2

Chen Ping cut meat fairly to share.
Even on that, the palace historian had
      something to say.
A lad north of River Wei before,
I am an old man south of the river today.
I shed tears in the autumn wind,
Joyous at the frontier furthest away.
Officials wind through palace gates.
Who pities a sick man who in the gorges
      has to stay?

昔遊

I

昔者與高李，晚登單父台。寒蕪際碣
石，萬里風雲來。桑柘葉如雨，飛藿
共徘徊。清霜大澤凍，禽獸有餘哀。
是時倉廩實，洞達寰區開。猛士思滅
胡，將帥望三台。君王無所惜，駕馭
英雄材。幽燕盛用武，供給亦勞哉。
吳門轉粟帛，泛海陵蓬萊。肉食三千
萬，獵射起黃埃。

II

隔河憶長眺，青崴已摧頹。不及少年
日，無復故人杯。賦詩獨流涕，亂世
想賢才。有能市駿骨，莫恨少龍媒。
商山議得失，蜀主脫嫌猜。呂尚封國
邑，傅説已鹽梅。景晏楚山深，水鶴
去低回。龐公任本性，攜子臥蒼苔。

Former Trips

I

Late, I climbed a terrace in Shanfu,
With Gao Shi and Li Bai, on a former
    day,
Overlooking stone tablets, on a cold
    wasteland,
With wind and cloud coming, from
    endless miles away.

Mulberry leaves fell like rain.
Flying blue licorice seemed to follow
    me on my way.
The big marsh was chilled with clear
    frost.
In a cheerless mood, fowl and beast
    were found to stay.

At that time, the granaries were full,
With the whole realm openly accessed.
Fierce warriors hoped to rid nomads.
Ideas of promotion were what generals
    addressed.

Our king held nothing back,
Supervising heroes of talent.
Warfare was frequent in Yan and You.
It was hard to have provisions sent.

From Wu, we got grain and silk,
Past isles like those of Penglai on the sea.
Three hundred thousand people were
    eating meat.
Hunting let yellow dust free.

II

I recall gazing long across Yellow River.
My youthful years have already reached
    a ruinous end.
Nothing matches the days of one's youth.
No more will there be drinks with an old
    friend.

I tear alone, writing poems
And, in an age of turmoil, think of
    sages with talent.
The rich can buy bones of famed horses.

Rare steeds are few, so do not lament.

Recluses at Shang Mountain discussed
    against serving brutal rulers.
Without suspicion, the bond a Shu king
    built could excel.
Lu Shang was enfeoffed a territory.
Fu Yue ruled his people well.

Cranes by waters hesitate on leaving.
Deep in Chu mountains, it is late in the
    day.
Pang Degong followed his nature as a
    recluse.
On green moss, he took his children
    and lay.

自瀼西荆扉且移居東屯茅屋四首，其一

白鹽危山北，赤甲古城東，平地一川穩，高山四面同。煙霜淒野日，梗稻熟天風。人事傷蓬轉，吾將守桂叢。

From my Humble House at River West, Temporarily Moving to a Thatched Cottage at East Camp, no 1

East of an old town named Red Shell,
My cottage is north of tall White Salt
  Mountain.
A river runs constantly across the flat
  land.
In all directions, similar images of high
  hills I gain.
Paddies are ready for harvesting in the
  wind.
Under the sun, mist and frost cover this
  gloomy, wild terrain.
I shall stay here with cassias as a recluse,
After human affairs have made me a
  tumbleweed, rolling in pain.

自瀼西荊扉且移居東屯茅屋四首，其二

東屯復瀼西，一種往青溪。來往皆茅
屋，淹留為稻畦。市喧宜近利，林僻
此無蹊。若訪衰翁語，須令贅客迷。

From my Humble House at River West, Temporarily Moving to a Thatched Cottage at East Camp, no 2

East Camp and River West
Are neighborhoods by a blue river in
   the same way.
Thatched cottages are everywhere.
Because of the paddies, I stay.
Close to the market, it is a noisy town.
To reach the remote woods, there is no
   pathway.
Should there be visitors for this weak,
   old man,
I need to let unneeded guests get astray.

自瀼西荊扉且移居東屯茅屋四首，其三

道北馮都使，高齋見一川。子能渠細石，吾亦沼清泉。枕帶還相似，柴荊即有焉。斫畬應費日，解纜不知年。

From my Humble House at River West, Temporarily Moving to a Thatched Cottage at East Camp, no 3

Feng, the capital's envoy, lives by a path
　　to the north,
Overlooking a stream from his study at a
　　height.
He can make a sluice of pebbles.
I too can pool up a spring that is clear.
We are alike in what we wear or use.
Beyond my brushwood gate, a river also
　　comes in sight.
I shall spend time on my cultivated plot.
To unmoor my boat, I know not which
　　year.

118

自瀼西荊扉且移居東屯茅屋四首，其四

牢落西江外，參差北戶閒。久游巴子宅，臥病楚人山。幽獨移佳境，清深隔遠關。寒空見鴛鷺，回首憶朝班。

From my Humble House at River West, Temporarily Moving to a Thatched Cottage at East Camp, no 4

Worn and forlorn, I live beyond River
    West.
Almost opposite, your home and my
    north door lie.
I have lain sick in the hills of Chu,
A long-term rover among Ba folks, as
    time goes by.
I have moved to a scenic, secluded spot.
Quiet and deep beyond passes, I form no
    human tie.
I recall processions for the dawn court
When I see mandarin ducks and egrets
    in the cold sky.

從驛次草堂復至東屯二首，其一

峽內歸田客，江邊借馬騎。非尋戴安
道，似向習家池。峽險風塵僻，天寒
橘柚垂。築場看斂積，一學楚人為。

From the Post-station, I Go to my Thatched Hut, then Back Again to East Camp, no.1

In the gorges, for a returnee to the fields,
A horse by the river is for me to borrow.
This is not a trip to seek Dai Andao,
   failed but fun,
Rather one for endless wine at Xi Pool
   years ago.
Tangerines and pomelos hang down on
   a cold day.
Over steep, remote gorges, dusty winds
   blow.
With a threshing-floor built, I look at
   the harvest.
Let me learn from the Chu people and
   follow.

從驛次草堂復至東屯二首，其二

短景難高臥，衰年強此身。山家蒸栗暖，野飯射麋新。世路知交薄，門庭畏客頻。牧童斯在眼，田父實為鄰。

From the Post-station, I Go to my Thatched Hut, then Back Again to East Camp, no.2

I drag myself along in my waning years,
Hard to sleep tight with shorter daylight
  overhead.
Warm, steamed chestnuts from a hillside
  home and peasant rice
Go with venison of a deer just shot dead.
Friendship is casual in this world.
Often, guests at my door give me dread.
Farmers are truly my neighbors.
Herd boys are in view right ahead.

園人送瓜

江閒雖炎瘴，瓜熟亦不早。柏公鎮夔
國，滯務茲一掃。食新先戰士，共少
及溪老。傾筐蒲鴿青，滿眼顏色好。
竹竿接嵌竇，引注來鳥道。沈浮亂水
玉，愛惜如芝草。落刃嚼冰霜，開懷
慰枯槁。許以秋蒂除，仍看小童抱。
東陵跡蕪絕，楚漢休征討。園人非故
侯，種此何草草？

A Gardener Sends me Melons

Though hot and miasmal by the river,
Ripe melons are still in delay.
Under Lord Bo in Kuizhou,
The habit of leaving things undone is
    swept away.
Fresh melons first go to soldiers,
Then some to the young and a creekside
    old man like me.
Put in reed baskets, like green pigeons,
They look pleasing absolutely.
Joined bamboo poles set in burrows

Conduct water over a precipitous way.
Jade-like melons that randomly float or
    sink in water
Are valued like the immortals' lingzi.
Chopped open, they taste like ice and
    frost,
Give me joy and help my body in decay.
He can tell as stalks come off in fall,
They will make armfuls for children
    that all can see.
Wars between Chu and Han have ended.
Gone is the famed melon grower of
    a former day.
Why did this gardener plunge into
    melon growing?
He is not another defeated Count of
    Dongling of yesterday.

暮春題瀼西新賃草屋五首，其一

久嗟三峽客，再與暮春期。百舌欲無
語，繁花能幾時。谷虛雲氣薄，波亂
日華遲。戰伐何由定，哀傷不在玆。

In Late Spring, on my Newly Rented Thatched Cottage at River West, no.1

I sigh for long as a guest of the Three
   Gorges.
Late spring has a date with me again.
The shrike, called "A Hundred
   Tongues" is almost speechless.
How long can floral glory remain?

In the empty valley, clouds look thin.
On rough waves, sunbeams slowly wane.
How can wars be settled?
Here I get relief from grief and pain.

暮春題瀼西新賃草屋五首，其二

此邦千樹橘，不見比封君。養拙干戈
際，全生麋鹿群。畏人江北草，旅食
瀼西雲。萬里巴渝曲，三年實飽聞。

In Late Spring, on my Newly Rented Thatched Cottage at River West, no.2

From this land of myriad tangerine trees,
I do not see any count with a fief appear.
In war, I practice "Ineptitude", the
    lifestyle of Tao Qian,
Preserving my life among herds of deer.
Like the clouds of River West, I live as a
    wanderer.
Like the grass north of the river, of
    people I am in fear.
Countless miles away, for three years,
I have more than enough songs of Ba
    and Yu to hear.

暮春題瀼西新賃草屋五首，其三

彩雲陰復白，錦樹曉未青。身世雙蓬
鬢，乾坤一草亭。哀歌時自短，醉舞
為誰醒。細雨荷鋤立，江猿吟翠屏。

In Late Spring, on my Newly Rented Thatched Cottage at River West, no.3

At dawn, trees like brocade look green.
Colorful clouds again turn white in the
    shadow.
Between Heaven and Earth, I live in a
    thatched pavilion.
With disheveled hair, I spend my life on
    this land.
I dance when drunk, but for whom
    should I be sober?
I fault myself when I sing in sorrow.
Riverside gibbons call by verdant cliffs.
In a drizzle, holding a hoe I stand.

暮春題瀼西新賃草屋五首，其四

壯年學書劍，他日委泥沙。事主非無
祿，浮生即有涯。高齋依藥餌，絕域
改春華。喪亂丹心破，王臣未一家。

In Late Spring, on my Newly Rented Thatched Cottage at River West, no.4

In my prime, I studied books, practicing
    on my sword,
Which later with mud and sand, got
    thrown away.
I shall get ashore from my drifting life.
From my employers, I am not without
    pay.
I rely on medicinal herbs in my high
    study.
This outpost looks different in spring.
My loyalty breaks in death and turmoil.
As his staff, I have no familial bond
    with the king.

暮春題瀼西新賃草屋五首，其五

欲陳濟世策，已老尚書郎。為息豺虎
鬥，空慚鴛鷺行。時危人事急，風逆
羽毛傷。落日悲江漢，中霄淚滿床。

In Late Spring, on my Newly Rented Thatched Cottage at River West, no.5

I wished to offer plans to save the age.
Already old, I am just a secretary by
    name.
Wars with rebels have not stopped.
Palace officials in processions put me to
    shame.
In peril, all human affairs are urgent.
Like a bird with damaged feathers in
    upwind, I appear.
I grieve by Yangzi and Han at sunset.
By midnight, all out in bed I tear.

題忠州龍興寺所居院壁

忠州三峽内，井邑聚雲根。小市常爭
米，孤城早閉門。空看過客淚，莫覓
主人恩。淹泊仍愁虎，深居賴獨園。

Inscribed on the Wall of the Compound where I Stayed in Longxing Temple at Zhongzhou

Zhongzhou, within the three gorges,
Has towns clustered near a mountain.
In small markets, people fight to get rice.
Locking their gates early is a habit they
　　maintain.

Seek not the kindness of a host.
Tears of this wanderer are shed in vain.
I still worry about tigers, lingering here,
Relying on the free food from a temple
　　that I may obtain.

晚

杖藜尋晚巷，灸背近牆喧。人見幽居
僻，吾知拙養尊。朝廷問府主，耕稼
學山村。歸翼飛棲定，寒燈亦閉門。

Late in the Day

With a pigweed staff, I go down the lane
   late.
To sun my back, a space near the warm
   wall I fill.
Others see my home as remote and quiet.
I value a lifestyle of "Ineptitude", simple
   and tranquil.

For matters with the court, I consult the
   local chief
And learn farming from villagers by the
   hill.
I shut my gate in the cold with a lamp
As birds return to roost and become still.

小園

由來巫峽水，本自楚人家。客病留因
藥，春深買為花。秋庭風落果，瀼岸
雨頹沙。問俗營寒事，將詩待物華。

Little Garden

The waters of Wu Gorges, from the start,
From the Chu land, begin to flow.
I stay for medicinal herbs as a sick guest.
In late spring, buying blooms is what I
  follow.
Rain makes sandbanks of rivers slide.
In fall yards, fruits drop as winds blow.
I write poems to wait for another cycle
  of flowering,
In quest for ways to winter here, as local
  customs go.

長江兩首，其一

眾水會涪萬，瞿塘爭一門。朝宗人共
挹，盜賊爾誰尊。孤石隱如馬，高蘿
垂飲猿。歸心異波浪，何事即飛翻。

The Long River, no.1

Many rivulets meet at Fu and Wan.
At Qutang Gorge, they vie for the same
　　gateway.
To honor our ancestors, we all pour
　　wine.
In showing their respects, to whom do
　　robbers convey?
Gibbons hung from high creepers reach
　　down to drink.
A horse-like, solitary rock is out of the
　　way.
My homesick heart differs from waves.
What makes it so turbulent right away?

長江兩首，其二

浩浩終不息，乃知東極臨。眾流歸海
意，萬國奉君心。色借瀟湘潤，聲驅
灩澦深。未辭添霧雨，接上遇衣襟。

The Long River, no.2

Recognizing the eastern extremity,
Currents of the big river never wane.
Returning to the sea is the wish of all
　　streams.
To serve the king is the consensus of
　　each domain.
It borrows colors from Xiao and Xiang.
A shrill pitch past deep Yanyu Rocks, it
　　can sustain.
Landing on your lapels will be drops
Of the extra, unstoppable mist and rain.

孟倉曹步趾領新酒醬二物滿器見遺老大

楚岸通秋屐，胡床面夕畦。籍糟分汁
滓，甕醬落提攜。飯糲添香味，朋來
有醉泥。理生那免俗，方法報山妻。

Meng of the Granaries Section Comes on Foot to Give this Old Man Full Pots of New Wine and Bean Sauce

I face the fields on my nomad couch
    after sunset.
In fall, there is a through passage along
    the Chu shore.
Your bean paste in jars spills in
    transportation.
The wine has been filtered from the lees.
Friends who come get fully drunk.
After cooking, the fragrance of my
    unpolished rice is more.
How can one avoid everyday matters in
    life?
Share your recipe with my wife, please.

八月十五夜月二首，其一

滿目飛明鏡，歸心折大刀。轉蓬行地遠，攀桂仰天高。水路疑霜雪，林棲見羽毛。此時瞻白兔，直欲數秋毫。

The Moon on the Night of the Fifteenth of the Eighth Month, no.1

Like the sword's broken ring, I cannot
    return home in full circle.
The moon is a clear mirror in flight.
I travel afar, resembling a tumbleweed.
For the cassia in the moon, I watch it at
    a height.

The moonlit river seems covered by
    frost and snow.
Feathers of birds roosting in forests
    come in sight.
If I gaze at White Hare of the moon,
I can count its fine hair, however slight.

八月十五夜月二首，其二

稍下巫山峽，猶銜白帝城。氣沈全浦暗，輪仄半樓明。刁斗皆催曉，蟾蜍且自清。張弓倚殘魄，不獨漢家營。

The Moon on the Night of the Fifteenth of the Eighth Month, no.2

Coming down a little above Wu Gorge,
The moon still holds Baidi City in its
   light.
With less vigor, the whole shore is dark.
The orb aslant makes half the tower
   bright.

Watch rattles all hasten dawn.
The Toad in the moon cannot stay
   upright.
Not just in the camps of the Han empire,
We can see soldiers stretch bows under
   waning moonlight.

峽口二首，其一

峽口大江閒，西南控百蠻。城欹連粉
堞，岸斷更青山。開闢多天險，防隅
一水關。亂離聞鼓角，秋氣動衰顏。

The Mouth of the Gorges, no.1

In the big river, boulders forming the
    gorge's mouth appear.
To peace on our terms, a hundred
    southwestern tribes adhere.
Whitewashed battlements conjoin the
    city wall aslant.
At the shore's end, green hills reappear.
The gorge is a water gate for defense,
One of the many natural barriers our
    Creator left here.
Autumn blasts strike at my worn face.
A refugee from wars, beats of bugle and
    drum I hear.

峽口二首，其二

時清關失險，世亂戟如林。去矣英雄
事，荒哉割據心。蘆花留客晚，楓樹
坐猿深。疲苶煩親故，諸侯數賜金。

The Mouth of the Gorges, no.2

At peace, the gorge is a barrier no more.
In turmoil, pikes resemble a forest.
Gone are the deeds of heroes.
Wasted are schemes of warlords put to
  rest.
Gibbons sit deep into maple trees.
By reed flowers, I am a long detained
  guest.
Weary and bored, I trouble my old
  relatives and friends,
Often for money from officials, at my
  request.

東屯月夜

抱疾漂萍老，防邊舊穀屯。春農親異
俗，歲月在衡門。青女霜楓重，黃牛
峽水喧。泥留虎鬥跡，月掛客愁村。
喬木澄稀影，輕雲倚細根。數驚聞雀
噪，暫睡想猿蹲。日轉天花白，風來
北斗昏。天寒不成寢，無夢有歸魂。

Moonlit Night at East Camp

Old and sick, I am a floating duckweed,
At a grain-producing camp, for self-
    defense in a yesteryear.
I go by strange customs here, in spring
    farming.
Behind shut gates, I pass each month
    and year.

Frost Goddess makes maples heavy.
At Yellow Ox Gorge, noisy waters flow.
Mud retains the tracks of tigers fighting.
A wanderer in a moonlit village is in
    sorrow.

Tall trees cast clear, sparse shadows.
Light clouds rest along a small hill.
I imagine gibbons crouching in my nap.
The often startling ruckus raised by
　　sparrows hangs on still.

As the sun rolls, the east looks bright.
The North Dipper fades as winds come.
I cannot fall asleep in the cold.
The dreamless soul yearns for home.

入宅三首，其一

奔峭背赤甲，斷崖當白鹽。客居愧遷
次，春色漸多添。花亞欲移竹，鳥窺
新卷簾。衰年不敢恨，睠概欲相兼。

Moving into my Cottage, no.1

With Red Shell behind and White Salt
　　in front,
I moved near sharp cliffs in this terrain.

A guest resident feels shamed for
　　moving often.
In time, more spring colors I can gain.
I want to move bamboos away from
　　flowering branches.
Birds peer in past my newly rolled-
　　up curtain.
Since I wish to meet those I care for,
I dare not resent my health on the wane.

入宅三首，其二

亂後居難定，春歸客未還。水生魚復
浦，雲暖麝香山。半頂梳頭白，過眉
拄杖斑。相看多使者，一一問函關。

Moving into my Cottage, no.2

After the turmoil, it is hard to decide
　　where to live.
The wanderer has not returned when
　　spring is here again.
Waters rise at Yufu Shore.

Clouds muffle Shexiang Mountain.
As I comb, half my head is white.
I lean on a tall, mottled cane.
Those I see mostly have a mission.
To news of Hangu Pass, their questions
pertain.

入宅三首，其三

宋主歸州宅，雲通白帝城。吾人淹老
病，旅食豈才名。峽口風常急，江流
氣不平。只應與兒子，飄轉任浮生。

Moving into my Cottage, no.3

Clouds link me at White Emperor City
With Song Yu's house at Guizhou of a
former year.
Old and sick, I am on a wanderer's fare.
With his talent and fame, I cannot
compare.
The river's current has not gone down.
At the gorge's mouth, fast winds always

blow.
All I should do is to drift with my son,
On a turbulent voyage of life and let go.

第五弟豐，獨在江左，近三四載，寂
無消息，覓使寄此，二首，其一

亂後嗟吾在，羈棲見汝難。草黃馿驥
病，沙晚鶺鴒寒。楚設關城險，吳吞
水府寬。十年朝夕淚，衣袖不曾乾。

**My Fifth Younger Brother, Feng, has
been Living Alone on the Left of
River Yangzi, for Three or Four
Years, without any News. I Send my
Poems to him through a Messenger,
no.1**

A detained wanderer finds it hard to see
you.
After the war, I sigh though I have not
died.
Rare horses sicken as grass turns yellow.

143

Like wagtails, close brothers get chilled
   on sands by eventide.
Leaving Chu and its passes is perilous.
You are in Wu, surrounded by waters,
   far and wide.
For ten years I tear by day and night.
My sleeves have not dried.

第五弟豐，獨在江左，近三四載，寂
無消息，覓使寄此，二首，其二

聞汝依山寺，杭州定越州。風塵淹別
日，江漢失清秋。影著啼猿樹，魂飄
結蜃樓。明年下春水，東盡白雲求。

**My Fifth Younger Brother, Feng, has
been Living Alone on the Left of
River Yangzi, for Three or Four
Years, without any News. I Send my
Poems to him through a Messenger,
no.2**

I heard of your stay in a hillside temple,

In Hangzhou or Yuezhou over there.
Cool Fall has gone at Yangzi and Han.
Days of our parting lengthen in the wind
   and dust of warfare.
I reside where gibbons cry amid trees.
For you in a mirage, my mind and soul
   care.
I shall go east for you where white
   clouds end,
On a voyage in spring next year.

刈稻了詠懷

稻穫空雲水，川平對石門。寒風疏草
木，旭日散雞豚。野哭初聞戰，樵歌
稍出村。無家問消息，作客信乾坤。

My Thoughts after a Rice Harvest

The level stream faces a stone gate.
They harvest rice after the rain clears.
Few grass and trees face the cold wind.
Chickens and pigs scatter as the dawn

sun appears.

Woodcutters' songs slowly emerge from villages.

People weep in the open when news of war come to their ears.

I have none to ask for information.

Towards believing in Heaven, a wanderer's mind steers.

夜

露下天高秋氣清，空山獨夜旅魂驚。
疏燈自照孤帆宿，新月猶懸雙杵鳴。
南菊再逢人臥病，北書不至雁無情。
步簷倚杖看牛斗，銀漢遙應接鳳城。

Night

Under a dewy, cloudless fall sky,

At a deserted, airy hill alone at night, a wanderer is in fright.

The new moon stays; pounding pestles make noise.

I have a weak lamp and solitary sail
overnight.
Chrysanthemums of the south bloom
again when I lie sick.
The callous wild goose and letters from
the north are out of sight.
Under the eaves, on a cane I watch two
stars: Niu and Dou.
The Milky Way should join Changnan
afar from this site.

東屯北崦

盜賊浮生困，誅求異俗貧。空村惟見
鳥，落日未逢人。步壑風吹面，看松
露滴身。遠山回白首，戰地有黃塵。

North Mountain by East Camp

Due to rebels, hardships hold a drifter
in an embrace.
Exactions have impoverished the base,
strange populace.

I see only birds in deserted villages.
At sunset, of people there is not a trace.
Dews drip on me as I look at pines.
When I pace the ravine, a wind blows on
my face.
I turn my white-haired head to distant
mountains.
On battlefields, yellow dust is in every
place.

簡吳郎司法

有客乘舸自忠州，遣騎安置瀼西頭。
古堂本買藉疏豁，借汝遷居停宴遊。
雲石熒熒高葉曙，江風颯颯亂帆秋。
卻為姻婭過逢地，許坐曾軒數散愁。

A Note to Legal Administrator Wu

From Zhongzhou on a large boat is my
guest,
Who gets a ride from me and lodging at
River West.

I bought the old cottage for its ample
    space.
As you move in, I shall have my feasts
    suppressed.

Clouds and rocks glint through tall
    trees at dawn.
In fall, with noisy winds on the river,
    sails cannot keep abreast.
It is for my in-laws to get together here.
Let me sit in the studio and put my
        sorrow to rest.

九月一日過孟十二倉曹十四主薄兄弟

藜杖侵寒露，蓬門啓曙煙。力稀經樹
歇，老困撥書眠。秋覺追隨盡，來因
孝友偏。清談見滋味，爾輩可忘年。

**On the First Day of the Ninth Month,
Stopping by the Home of Meng, the
Twelfth, of the Granaries Section and**

his Brother, the Fourteenth, Assistant Magistrate

My humble gate opens to dawn mist.
On my pigweed staff, I brave cold dew,
    though hard pressed.
I doze off with open books, being old
    and drowsy.
Weak, I stop by a tree to rest.
Social visits are over in fall,
But for your extreme friendliness and
    brotherhood expressed.
Despite our age difference, we bond.
Our conversations are held with interest.

七月一日題終明府水樓二首，其一

高棟曾軒已自涼，秋風此日灑衣裳。
翛然欲下陰山雪，不去非無漢署香。
絕壁過雲開錦繡，疏松夾水奏笙簧。
看君宜著王喬履，真賜還疑出尚方。

150

On the First Day of the Seventh Month, Inscribed on the Water Pavilion of County Chief Zhong, no.1

This layered pavilion with high beams
    can keep heat away.
My robe gets blown by fall winds today.
Suddenly, sunless hills threaten to snow.
Ready for the palace, you choose to stay.
Clouds across cliffs leave traces like
    embroidered brocade.
Rain through sparse pines sounds like
    panpipes in play.
Like a real endowment, it may well be
    the work of palace artisans.
You are in the magic shoes of Wang
    Qiao, an immortal of yesterday.

七月一日題終明府水樓二首，其二

宓子彈琴邑哉日，終軍棄繻英妙時。
承家節操尚不泯，為政風流今在茲。

151

可憐賓客盡傾蓋，何處老翁來賦詩。
楚江巫峽半雲雨，清簟疏簾看弈棋。

On the First Day of the Seventh Month, Inscribed on the Water Pavilion of County Chief Zhong, no.2

Mizi governed well though he played
    the zither all day.
For Changan, Zhong Jun threw his re-
    entry permit away.
You show charisma in management
    right here.
In you, the high principle and tradition
    of your family stay.
Your lovely guests all tilt towards one
    another to talk.
Why this old man comes to write poems,
    I cannot say.
On a cool mat by open-weave drapes,
    I watch games of chess,
With River Chu and Wu Gorge under
    cloud and rain half-way.

又上後園山腳

I

昔我游山東，憶戲東嶽陽。窮秋立日
觀，矯首望八荒。朱崖著毫髮，碧海
吹衣裳。蓐收困用事，玄冥蔚強梁。
逝水自朝宗，鎮石各其方。平原獨憔
悴，農力廢耕桑。非關風露凋，曾是
戍役傷。於時國用富，足以守邊疆。

II

朝廷任猛將，遠奪戎虜場。到今事反
復，故老淚萬行。龜蒙不復見，況乃
懷舊鄉。肺萎屬久戰，骨出熱中腸。
哀逼遠征人，去家死路旁。不及父祖
塋，累累塚相當。

Once again Climbing the Base of the Mountain by my Rear Garden

On my trip to Shandong in the past,
I frolicked on the south slope of East

153

Mount, I recall.
I lifted my head for the wilds around me
And stood on Summer Terrace all fall.

I could see details from a red cliff.
My robe got the wind from the blue sea.
Rushou, Lord of Autumn, barely did his
    job.
Xuanming, Lord of Winter, had vigor in
    plenty.

With waters all flowing towards their
    Origin,
Guardian rocks for all directions came in
    view.
Plains looked singularly dreary.
Farming and sericulture did not continue.

Wind and dew weakened not the state.
Garrison duties brought people pain.
At that time, the empire stayed wealthy.
Peace at borders could remain.

II

The court assigned fierce generals
To seize nomads' territories far away.
All old people cried a river
As war outcomes turned the other way.

Mount Gui and Meng are not seen again.
Moreover, homesickness is on my mind.
Lung disease is a protracted battle.
Bone spurs and heat in my bowels are
    what I find.

Worried, with a cane and a sword,
I climb a mound, north of the grove.
Birds and gibbons hide in the miasmal,
    poisonous air.
The gorge is dry, with the yellow south
    sun above.

Headwater has come to Yangzi and Han.
Autumn winds have begun.
In my wish to climb and go somewhere,
I face a stream bridgeless and overrun.

I sadden over men on distant campaigns,
Who, far from home, die by the roadside.

They cannot return to their family
cemeteries,
Where rows and rows of tombs lie side
side.

課小豎鋤斫舍北果林，枝蔓荒穢，淨
訖移床三首，其一

病枕依茅棟，荒鉏淨果林。背堂資僻
遠，在野興清深。山雉防求敵，江猿
應獨吟。泄雲高不去，隱几亦無心。

**Overseeing my Servant in Hoeing and
Pruning the Fruit Orchard, North of
the Cottage, where Overgrown
Branches and Creepers had a Blight.
On Completion, I Moved my Couch
there, no.1**

In my thatched cottage, I lie sick on my
pillow.
A hoe is used to rid the fruit orchard's
blight.

With my back to the hall, I gain
    remoteness.
The wilds give me deep, pure delight.
Riverside gibbons respond to my
    chanting alone.
Hillside pheasants fend off those
    seeking a fight.
I am a recluse with no will to leave,
Like stagnant clouds at a height.

課小豎鋤斫舍北果林，枝蔓荒穢，淨
訖移床三首，其二

眾壑生寒早，長林卷霧齊。青蟲懸就
日，朱果落封泥。薄俗防人面，全身
學馬蹄。吟詩坐回首，隨意葛中低。

**Overseeing my Servant in Hoeing and
Pruning the Fruit Orchard, North of
the Cottage, where Overgrown
Branches and Creepers had a Blight.**

On Completion, I Moved my Couch there, no.2

Tall forests fully in fog look uniform.
Ravines soon let chilling effects show.
Red fruits fall and get embedded in mud.
Sunbeams make hanging green insects
  follow.
I guard against deceit, in a land of base
  morals,
And study hard "Horse's Hoofs", a book
  of wisdom of Zhuangzi long ago.
On chanting poems, I sit and look back,
Freely letting my kudzu hat slip down
  low.

課小豎鋤斫舍北果林，枝蔓荒穢，淨
訖移床三首，其三

籬弱門何向，沙虛岸只摧。日斜魚更
食，客散鳥還來。寒水光難定，秋山
響易哀。天涯稍曛黑，倚杖更徘徊。

Overseeing my Servant in Hoeing and Pruning the Fruit Orchard, North of the Cottage, where Overgrown Branches and Creepers had a Blight. On Completion, I Moved my Couch there, no.3

The bank made of loose sand crumbles.
By a weak fence, where my gate faces
   I am not certain.
Birds return when guests have left.
At sunset, fish feed again.
Sunlight on cold waters easily scatters.
Fall sounds tend to be sad from the
   mountain.
Darkness comes faintly from the horizon.
I linger all the more on my cane.

瞿塘兩崖

三峽傳何處，雙崖壯此門。入天猶石
色，穿水忽雲根。猱玃須髯古，蛟龍
窟宅尊。羲和冬馭近，愁畏日車翻。

159

The Paired Cliffs of Qutang Gorge

Where do they say are the "Three
    Gorges"?
The twin cliffs, like a gate, make a grand
    sight.
The base in water, called "Roots of
    Cloud" is the bottom of a mountain.
The top has the color of rocks, piercing
    the sky at a height.
Here are gibbons of ancient origin with
    yellow hair,
With respected flood dragons and their
    caves on site.
In winter, drivers of the sun, Zi and He,
    get near.
An overturned carriage of the sun gives
    me fright.

瞿塘懷古

西南萬壑注，劫敵兩崖開。地與山根
裂，江從月窟來。削成當白帝，空曲
隱陽臺。疏鑿功雖美，陶鈞力大哉。

Recalling the Past at Qutang Gorge

Like fierce foes, two cliffs stand apart,
With torrents from myriad ravines
    draining from the southwest.
The river starts from the moon's cave,
With the ground from the mountain base
    split when stressed.
Facing White Emperor City, it was
    carved,
With warped spaciousness, able to keep
    Sun Terrace recessed.
Though King Yu's dredging is beautiful,
Great indeed is the Creator's force
    expressed.

赤甲

卜居赤甲遷居新，兩見巫山楚水春。
灸背可以獻太子，美芹由來知野人。
荊州鄭薛寄書近，蜀客郗岑非我鄰。
笑接郎中評事飲，病從深酌道吾真。

Red Shell Cliff

Lately I moved to Red Shell Cliff.
Twice, spring scenes of Mount Wu and
　　Chu river come in sight.
My back-sunning skills are presentable
　　to a prince.
Getting fine celery relies on a rustic's
　　foresight.
Zheng and Xue of Jingzhou recently
　　wrote to me.
Xi and Cen, guests of Shu, are not
　　neighbors at my site,
I smile and accept wine from the
　　director and judge.
Though sick, after many cups, I tell
　　what is forthright.

反照

反照開巫峽，寒空半有無。已低魚復
暗，不盡白鹽孤。荻岸如秋水，松門
似畫圖。牛羊識童僕，既夕應傳呼。

Reflected Sunlight

Reflected sunbeams expose Wu Gorge.
Only half of the cold sky receives light.
Endless White Salt Cliff stands alone.
Yufu Bank, already low, is again not
     bright.
Reeds by the shore resemble fall waters.
Picturesque, door-like pines come in
     sight.
Cattle recognize herd boys,
Responding to their calls at twilight.

憑孟倉曹將書覓土婁舊莊

平居喪亂後，不到洛陽岑。為歷雲山
閒，無辭荊棘深。北風黃葉下，南浦
白頭吟。十載江湖客，茫茫遲暮心。

Relying on Meng of the Granaries Section to Take a Letter and Seek out my Old Estate at Tulou

In peace after death and destruction,
To the peaks of Luoyang, I have yet to
    go.
For the estate, you will be at cloudy hills.
Amid deep brambles, this mission you
    will not forego.
White-haired on south shores, I chant
Under yellow leaves as winds blow.
Dazed in my late waning years,
I have been a wanderer since ten years
    ago.

除架

束薪已零落，瓠葉轉蕭疏。幸結白花
了，寧辭青蔓除。秋蟲聲不去，暮雀
意何如。寒事今牢落，人生亦有初。

Removing a Trellis

Gourd leaves are wilted and sparse
As tied sticks of a trellis are falling apart.
White flowers have luckily fruited.
With green vines, why can they not part?
The sound of fall insects has not gone.
What do twilight birds want at heart?
In the cold, everything is bleak and bare.
All in life end in death from the start.

奉贈蕭十二使君

I

昔在嚴公幕，俱為蜀使臣。艱危參大府，前後問清塵。起草鳴先路，乘槎動要津。王霑聊暫出，蕭雉只相馴。終始任安義，荒蕪孟母鄰。聯翩匍匐禮，意氣死生親。張老存家事，嵇康有故人。食恩慚鹵莽，鏤骨抱酸辛。巢許山林志，夔龍廊廟珍。鵬圖仍矯翼，熊軾且移輪。

II

磊落衣冠地，蒼茫土木身。壎篪鳴自合，金石瑩逾新。重憶羅江外，同游錦水濱。結歡隨過隙，懷日益沾巾。曠絕含香舌，稽留伏枕辰。停驂雙闕早，囘雁五湖春。不達長卿病，從來原憲貧。

Respectfully Presented to Governor Xiao, the Twelfth

I

Both as Lord Yan's subordinates in Shu,
We worked in his headquarters years
    ago.
In peril, we labored to manage the place.
First you were cut off from his moral
    leadership, and I now follow.

Early on, recognized as a writer of drafts,
As if on a fairy's raft, to a high post you
    could go.
Briefly you served as a county judge.
Like Xiao Zhiwei, you are the director
    of a bureau.

You care about Yan's mother.
Like Ren An, righteousness is your
    motto.
You crawl to pay respects in Yan's
    funeral.
In life and death, friendliness you show.

Like Old Zhang, you are concerned
   about his family.
An old friend raised Ji Kang's son; you
   will take Yan's son in also.
Unable to repay Yan, I am shamed by
   my rashness.
With guilt etched in my bones, I am
   in deep sorrow.

Like Ge Chaofu and Xu You, I like
   hill and forest.
Like Kui and Long, in the palace Hall of
   Fame, your esteem will grow.
I still plan to use the strong wings of a
   roc.
In your exalted post, you will use a bear
   on your carriage as a logo.

II

You are open to the public, among caps
   and gowns.
I am obscure and lost, stuck in soil and
   wood below.

Like Xun and Chi, we sound off in the
    same tempo.
Like metal and stone, we offer fresher
    notes in duo.

We toured outside Luoyang and by
    Brocade River.
These scenes in my memory can echo.
Our joyous outings passed quickly.
My kerchief gets more tears of
    homesickness and woe.

I cannot have an audience with the king.
Well detained here, I spend time lying
    on my pillow.
At the double palace gates, you stop
    your carriage early.
Like a homebound wild goose in spring,
    retiring in the Five Lakes is my credo.

Like Changqing, I am sick and a failure.
Like Yuan Xian, I am always poor as we
    know.
In the same plight as a fish caught on a
    wheel rut,

From the Count of Jianhe, I trust there
should be grains to borrow.

奉送魏六丈佑少府子交廣

I

賢家贊經綸，功成空名垂。子孫不振
耀，歷代皆有之。鄭公四葉孫，長大
常苦饑。眾中見毛骨，猶是麒麟兒。
磊落貞觀事，致君樸直詞。家聲蓋六
合，行色何其微。遇我蒼梧陰，忽驚
會面稀。議論有餘地，公侯來未遲。
虛思黃金貴，自笑青雲期。長卿久病
渴，武帝元同時。季子黑貂敝，得無
妻嫂欺。尚為諸侯客，獨屈州縣卑。

II

南遊炎海甸，浩蕩從此辭。窮途仗神
道，世亂輕土宜。解帆歲雲暮，可與

170

春風歸。出入朱門家，華屋刻蛟螭。
玉食亞王者，樂張遊子悲。侍婢艷傾
城，綃綺輕霧霏。掌中琥珀鐘，行酒
雙逶迤。新歡繼明燭，梁棟星辰飛。
兩情顧盼合，珠碧贈於斯。上貴見肝
膽，下貴不相疑。心事披寫間，氣酣
達所為。錯揮鐵如意，莫避珊瑚枝。
始兼邁逸興，終慎賓主儀。戎馬暗天
宇，嗚呼生別離。

Respectfully Seeing off Sheriff Wei Yu, the Sixth, Going to Jiaozhou and Guangzhou

I

A sage hero, you excel in your duties.
After success, what remains is just your
  name.
Your descendants are not prominent.
In every generation, it is the same.

The great grandson of duke of Zheng,
You grew up often hungry and forlorn.

171

In a crowd, from your physique,
You resemble the son of a unicorn.

Distinctly in the reign of Zhengguan,
Before the king, you honestly spoke.
Your family renown is spread all over.
But how simple are the preparations for
    traveling that you took.

We met at the north slope of Mount
    Cangwu,
At once shocked by our reunions so
    rare.
In discussions, you avoid extremes.
About a noble's title, you do not care.

Dear gold from palace recruitments is
    in vain for me.
I jeer at myself for missing blue clouds
    of the skies.
Like Sima Xiangru with diabetes, I am
    sick for a long time.
King Wu found Xiangru was in his era,
    to his pleasant surprise.

Su Qin's black sables were in disrepair.
Snubs from his wife and sister-in-law
   he could not avoid.
You are still a guest of the regional lords,
In low county positions, to fill a void.

II

You travel south to the torrid wilds.
For your big venture, from here you start.
At the roadblock of life, rely on the
   teachings of Heaven.
In troubled times, do not take primitive
   customs to heart,

Lowering your sail at the year's end,
Can you return in the spring breeze?
In grand mansions with carved dragons
   and vermilion gates,
You can come and go as you please.

With food better than that for princes
And music to the wanderer's sorrow,
You will have maids of peerless beauty
And dancers with silk ribbons like light

mist in snow.

You hold a flask like amber.
Two servants ply with wine the whole
    day.
With novel amusements and bright
    candles,
In a sober state, you cannot stay.

Two lovers unite starting with a glance.
Pearl and jade are given as a present.
Lovers value deep sincerity more
Than mutual suspicions being absent.

Lovers write to reveal their hearts.
Emotional people do what they will.
If you by mistake end a relationship,
Go on for a better one still.

They start with big, refined interests
And end, like careful host and guest,
    as old husband and wife.
Warhorses darken the firmament.
O death, to be parted in life!

奉送韋中承之晉赴湖南

寵渥徵黃漸，權宜借寇頻。湖南安背
水，峽內憶行春。王室仍多故，蒼生
倚大臣。還將徐孺榻，處處待高人。

Respectfully Seeing off Vice Censor Wei Zhijin on his Way to Hunan

Much favored like Huang Ba, you are in
    time summoned by the king.
Like Kou Xun, your talent is what
    commoners want to borrow.
Hunan is secure with its back to waters.
Within the gorges, people recall your
    spring inspection years ago.
The monarchy still has many problems.
All rely on justice that a great minister
    can bestow.
Virtuous Xu Zhi was offered a couch
    when he met his supervisor.
A lofty man like you will be pampered
    wherever you go.

歸

束帶還騎馬，東西卻渡船。林中才有
地，峽外絕無天。虛白高人靜，喧卑
俗累牽。他鄉悅遲暮，不敢廢詩篇。

Returning

I ride my horse after tightening my sash.
A boat then takes me east to west.
Only in the forest do I find my space.
Beyond the gorges, there are no skies.
A quiet, lofty man is humble and pure.
I am held by loud, base and worldly ties.
To enjoy my old age on a strange land,
I dare not skip poetry for a rest.

暫往白帝復還東屯

復作歸田去，猶殘獲稻功。築場憐穴
蟻，拾穗許村童。落杵光輝白，除芒
子粒紅。加餐可扶老，倉廩慰飄蓬。

Returning to East Camp after Going to White Emperor City for a While

I return to my fields again.
Chores in harvesting the rice still remain.
I let village boys glean the fallen ears.
Building the thrashing floor, I pity ants
    in holes already lain.
Pestles split husks that look white with a
    sheen.
With the shell off, a red sheath covers
    each grain.
Eating more supports the aged.
From the granary, a wanderer's comfort
    I gain.

柴門

I

泛舟登瀼西，迴首望兩崖。東城乾旱
天，其氣如焚柴。長影沒窈窕，餘光
散唅呀。大江蟠嵌根，歸海成一家。

下衝割坤軸，竦壁攢鏌鋣。蕭颯灑秋色，氣昏霾日車。峽門自此始，最窄容浮查。禹功翊造化，疏鑿就攲斜。巨渠決太古，眾水為長蛇。風塵緲吳蜀，舟楫通鹽麻。

II

我今遠遊子，飄轉混泥沙。萬物附本性，約身不願奢。茅棟蓋一床，清池有餘花。濁醪與脫粟，在眼無咨嗟。山荒人民少，地僻日夕佳。貧病固其蒼，富貴任生涯。老於干戈際，宅幸蓬蓽遮。石亂上雲氣，杉清延月華。賞妍又分外，理愜夫何誇。足了垂百年，敢居高士差。書此豁平昔，迴首猶暮霞。

Scrapwood Gate

I

By boat I reach River West.

178

As I turn, I catch sight of cliffs in a pair.
East of the city, under a scorching sky,
Effects of lit firewood are in the air.

Tall shadows get deeply submerged.
Light scatters from the setting sun.
The big river coils around the solid base
    of a mountain.
Into the sea, all rivulets join to run.

Sheer cliffs resemble bundles of rare
    swords.
The plunge cuts cosmic grids that lay.
A haze blurs the sun's carriage.
The noisy wind sends fall colors in a
    spray.

The gorges start here.
It admits only a floating raft at its
    narrowest.
King Yu's efforts helped Heaven.
Drainage and dredging follow how
    slopes rest.

This huge sluice is pre-historic.

Like a long snake, all tributaries form
   one pathway.
Boats transport salt and hemp,
With wind and mist, over Wu and Shu,
   all the way.

II

I am now a wanderer from afar,
In mud and sand, tumbling along.
All creatures stick to their basic nature.
For luxury, my disciplined mind does
   not long.

I have one bed, under a thatched roof.
By a clear pond, many flowers lie.
With unfiltered wine and paddy,
I do not sigh.

The remoteness suits me, day and night.
At the deserted hills, residents are few.
Being sick and poor becomes my norm.
Wealth and fame may come before my
   life is through.

In war, I grow old, but by luck
There is a humble hut for cover I can go.
Above jumbled rocks hang cloud and
  mist.
Through sparse firs, moonbeams flow.

Enjoying the fine scenery is my bonus.
I need not brag; to reason I consent.
I dare not be among the lofty or exalted.
With my longevity near a hundred, I am
  content.
I turn my head to the clouds of twilight.
This is written to bare how my life is
  spent.

送孟十二倉曹赴東京選

君行別老親，此去苦家貧。藻鏡留連
客，江山憔悴人。秋風楚竹冷，夜雪
鞏梅春。朝夕高堂念，應宜彩服新。

Seeing off Meng, the Twelfth, of the Granaries Section for a Selection Procedure in the Eastern Capital

This departure brings hardship to your
poor family,
As you leave your old parents and go
away.
Passing hill and river may be exhausting.
Mirror-like lakes with duckweeds will
make you stay.
Fall winds chill bamboos in Chu.
Gong County has overnight snow and
plum blooms on a spring day.
All day your parents think of you.
Return and cheer them in Laolaizi's way.

豎子至

楂梨且綴碧，梅杏半傳黃。小子幽園
至，輕籠熟奈香。山風猶滿把，野露
及新嘗。欲寄江湖客，提攜日月長。

182

A Servant Boy Comes

Hawthorns and pears have patches in
    green.
Plums and apricots turn yellow halfway.
With a light basket of ripe, fragrant
    sand apples.
A boy from a secluded garden comes
    along.
Wilderness dew lends freshness to the
    taste.
Winds from hills come fully my way.
I want to give some to a wanderer on
    river and lake,
But hauling them each day and night
    takes too long.

晚晴吳郎見過北舍

圍畦新雨潤，愧子廢鋤來。竹枝交頭
柱，柴扉隔徑開。欲棲群鳥亂，未去
小童催。明日重陽酒，相迎自釀醅。

Under Late Sunset, Mister Wu Visits me at my North Cottage

I feel guilty you stopped hoeing to come.
Garden plots are moist with new rain.
My scrapwood gate far from the trail is
  open.
I get propped on a double-headed,
  bamboo cane.
Your boy urges you to leave as you
  linger.
For roosting twigs, birds act chaotic and
  uncertain.
Tomorrow for the wine of the Double
  Ninth Festival,
With my own twice-brewed and
  unstrained ale, I shall entertain.

瀼西寒望

水色含群動，朝光切太虛。年侵頻悵
望，興遠一蕭疏。猿掛時相學，鷗行
炯自如。瞿塘春欲至，定卜瀼西居。

A View of River West in the Cold

The waters show colors and moving
    creatures within.
The great void is penetrated by dawn
    light.
My interest traveling afar is now weak.
I often feel depressed by aging and what
    comes in sight.
Gibbons hang and often imitate one
    another.
Gulls look free and sharp in flight.
Spring will soon come to the Qutang
    Gorge.
At River West, I have chosen my
    resting site.

除草

草有害於人，曾何生阻修。其毒甚蜂
蠆，甚多彌道周。清晨步前林，江色
未散憂。芒刺在我眼，焉能待高秋。

185

霜露一霑凝，蕙葉亦難留。荷鋤先童
稚，日入仍討求。轉致水中央，豈無
雙釣舟。頑根易滋蔓，敢使依舊丘。
自茲藩籬曠，更覺松竹幽。茇夷不可
闕，疾惡信如讎。

Weeding

Weeds harm humans.
They hamper harvests from years ago.
Their poison is worse than bees and
    wasps.
Along roads, profusely they grow.

At dawn, as I walked in the woods in
    front.
The riverscape did not lessen my sorrow.
They are like thistles and thorns.
How can I wait until cloudless fall and
    be slow?

Once frosty dews on crops freeze,
Orchid leaves find it hard to grow.
At sunset I was still fighting weeds,
Ahead of my young boy with a hoe.

I have a fishing boat for two.
To the mid-stream, I let my trash go.
Their tough roots can easily propagate.
By my old hill, dare I let them regrow?

From my hedge comes a wider view.
The tranquil looks of pine and bamboo
  echo.
Weeding should not be omitted.
I strongly hate weeds, my real foe.

灩澦

灩澦既沒孤根深，西來水多愁太陰。
江天漠漠鳥雙去，風雨時時龍一吟。
舟人漁子歌回首，估客胡商淚滿襟。
寄語舟航惡年少，休翻鹽井橫黃金。

Yanyu

Yanyu rocks with their lone, deep root
  have sunk.

We worry too much rain from the west
    may appear.
Two birds fly off to the far horizon.
In frequent rainstorms, the humming of
    dragons we hear.
Fishermen and all hands on deck sing
    and turn their heads.
Merchants and nomad traders fully tear.
Let me tell the young, rash navigators to
    take care.
The spilled produce from salt wells will
    make your gold disappear.

Year 768-770

暮秋將歸秦留別湖南幕府親友

水潤蒼梧野，天高白帝秋。途窮那免
哭，身老不禁愁。大府才能會，諸公
德業優。北歸衝雨雪，誰憫敝貂裘。

About to Return to Qin in Late Autumn, I Take Leave of my Friends in the Hunan Headquarters

In cloudless fall, under the deity, White
    Emperor,
On vast waters by Cangwu's wild terrain,
I cannot help weeping at a roadblock of
    my life,
Sad that my body is on the wane.
In the big headquarters, a hub for the
    talented,
In virtue and achievements, all have
    their special gain.
Who will pity my tattered sable cape
As I return north, rushing through sheets
    of freezing rain?

長沙送李十一銜

與子避地西康州，洞庭相逢十二秋。
遠愧尚方曾賜履，竟非吾土倦登樓。

189

久存膠漆應難並，一辱泥塗遂晚收。
李杜齊名真忝竊，朔雲寒菊倍離憂。

At Changsha, Seeing off Li Xian, the Eleventh

At West Kangzhou, for refuge we have
chosen the site.
After twelve autumns, at Lake Dongting
we re-unite.
Afar I am ashamed of my performance
at the palace,
On this strange land, weary of watching
my hometown at a height.
Insulted and muddied in my life and
career, I retire now, though late.
Hard to match is our long period of
friendship sealed tight.
That Li Xian and Du Fu are equal in
fame is really unearned.
North clouds and cold chrysanthemums
double our sad plight.

公安送韋二少府匡贊

逍遙公俊世多賢，送爾維舟惜此筵。
念我能書數字至，將詩不必萬人傳。
時危兵甲黃塵裏，日短江湖白髮前。
古往今來皆涕淚，斷腸分手各風塵。

At Gongan, Seeing off Sheriff Wei Kuangzan, the Second

Descendants of "Free-Roaming Duke"
  are always wise.
I moor to see you off, cherishing
  this feast.
My poems need not be shown to
  countless people.
Write me some words in a letter if you
  care.
In dangerous wars, amid yellow dust,
I notice short days on river and lake, and
  my short hair.
After we part broken-hearted, we face
  our own challenges.
Now as before, weeping on leaving has
  never ceased.

蘇大侍禦渙，靜者也，旅於江側，凡是不交州府之客，人事都絕久矣。肩輿江浦，忽訪老夫舟楫，而已茶酒內，予請誦詩，肯吟數首，才力素壯，辭句動人。接對明日，憶其湧思雷出。書篋几杖之外，殷殷留金石聲。賦八韻記異，亦記老夫傾倒於蘇至矣

龐公不浪出，蘇氏今有之。再聞誦新作，突遇黃初時。乾坤幾反覆，揚馬宜同時。今晨清鏡中，勝食齋房芝。予髮喜卻變，白閒生黑絲。昨夜舟火滅，湘娥簾外悲。百靈未敢散，風波寒江遲。

Attendant Censor Su Huan, a Quiet Man, Lodges by the River, Usually Shut to Visitors from the Prefecture Government and other Associates.

Carried on a Palanquin by the Shore, he Suddenly Paid a Call on this Old Fellow's Boat. While Sipping Tea and Wine, I asked him to Chant his Recent Poems. He was Willing to Chant a Few which Showed his Pure, Strong Talent, with Attractive Diction. The Next Day, I Recalled his Surging, Thunderous Thoughts which were Expressed in the Rich Sounds of Metal and Stone, around my Bookcase, Table and Cane. I Composed Eight Couplets to Record the Wonderful Experience and the Extreme Admiration from this Old Man for Su

Peng Dagong, the scholar, did not die in
    vain.
We have Mister Su today as his peer.
I have also heard him chant his recent
    poems
Which top those in the Huangchu Reign
    that we hold dear.
Heaven and Earth at times have shifted

ground.
I wish with him, Yang Xiong and Sima
Xiangru would appear.
Better than eating the lingzi in my
vegetarian kitchen,
This morn, in my mirror, bright and
clear,
My hair has happily changed.
Amid white threads, black strands grow.
Last night, when the torch on the boat
went out,
Maidens of the Xiang River beyond the
drapes were in sorrow.
The many spirits that gathered dared not
leave.
On the cold river, wind and wave were
slow.

銅官渚守風

不夜楚帆落，避風湘渚閒。水耕先浸草，春火更燒山。早泊雲物晦，逆行波浪慳。飛來雙白鶴，過去杳難攀。

At Tongguan Isle, Harboring from a Blast

We moor amid isles of River Xiang in
a blast.
Sails are lowered before it is night.
Farmers flood their fields before tilling.
In spring, hill fires are in sight.
An upstream voyage is against waves.
Moored early, I find everything not
bright.
It is hard to climb onto two white cranes
coming close.
They are already afar in flight.

嶽麓山道林二寺行

I

玉泉之南麓山殊，道林林壑爭盤紆。
寺門高開洞庭野，殿腳插入赤沙湖。
五月寒風冷佛骨，六時天樂朝香爐。
地靈步步雪山草，僧寶人人滄海珠。
塔劫宮牆壯麗敵，香廚松道清涼俱。
蓮花交響共命鳥，金榜雙迴三足烏。
方丈涉海費時節，懸圃尋河知有無。
暮年且喜經行近，春日兼蒙暄暖扶。

II

飄然斑白身奚適，傍此煙霞茅可誅。
桃源人家易制度，橘洲田土仍膏腴。
潭府邑中甚淳古，太守庭內不喧呼。
昔遭衰世皆晦跡，今華樂園養微軀。
依止老宿亦未晚，富貴功名焉足圖。
久為謝客尋幽慣，細學周顒免興孤。
一重一掩吾肺腑，山鳥山花吾友于。
宋公放逐曾題壁，物色分留與老夫。

Ballad of Two Temples: Mount Yuelu and Daolin

I

South of Jade Spring Monastery, Mount
 Yuelu Temple is unique.
Woods and ravines near Daolin Temple
 entwine as if in a fight.
The gate of one temple opens to the
 wilds of Dongting.
With Red Sand Lake, the rear of the
 other hangs tight.

Cold winds in the fifth month chill
 Buddha's bones.
All day, heavenly music by incense
 burners runs free.
In this spiritual place, Snow Hill's grass
 is found at every step.
Every precious monk is a "Pearl of the
 Gray Sea"

By good smelling kitchens, paths
 through pines are equally cool.

Peerless pagodas and walls are imposing
    in design.
Amid lotus blooms is a chorus of
    djivandjiva birds.
Two golden plaques reflect sunshine.

A voyage to Fang Zhang, the immortals'
    isle, takes time,
Let alone after Xuan Pu by the river, the
    fairies' terrain.
In my waning years, I like trips nearby,
On warm noisy days in spring, with a
    cane.

II

Under mist and cloud, I cut thatch for
    my cottage.
Where am I headed, as a wanderer and
    white-haired man?
Fields on Tangerine Isle are still rich.
A journey to Peach Flower Stream is an
    easy plan.

The governor's courtyard is quiet.

In the city of Tanzhou, the culture is
    ancient, simple and sincere.
After generations of decline, all have
    retired to obscurity.
To nurse my humble self, I am with
    flowers on a happy land here.

It is not late to grow old, living in a
    temple.
How can pursuing fame and gain be
    worthwhile?
Long used to seek quietude like Xie
    Lingyun,
I should focus on my interest, in Zhou
    Yu's scholarly style.

My friends are hillside birds and flowers.
From folds and layers, I have bared my
    heart.
Song Zhiwan inscribed on a wall in
    exile.
Of his past, this old man has left a part.

聶耒陽以僕阻水書致酒肉療饑荒江。
詩得代懷興盡本韻。至縣呈聶令。陸
路去方田驛四十里舟行一日時屬江漲
泊於方田

耒陽馳尺素，見訪荒江渺。義士烈女
家，風流吾賢紹。昨見狄相孫，許公
人倫表。前期翰林後，屈跡縣邑小。
知我礙湍濤，半旬獲浩溔。麾下殺元
戎，湖邊有長旒。孤舟增鬱鬱，僻路
殊悄悄。側驚猿猱捷，仰羨鸛鶴矯。
禮過宰肥羊，愁當置清醥。人非西喻
蜀，興在北坑趙。方行郴岸靜，未話
長沙擾。崔師乞已至，澧卒用矜少。
問罪消息真，開顏憩亭沼。

**Because I was Held up by a Flood, Nie
of Leiyang Sent Wine and Meat with
a Letter to me on a Deserted River.
A Poem can Serve to Express my
Inspiration with Available Rhymes.
When I Reach the County Seat, I shall
Present it to Magistrate Nie. The**

Land Route is Forty Miles from the Fangtian Station, but by Boat it Takes only a Day. As the River is Flooding now, I moor at Fangtian.

From Leiyang, a letter came in haste,
To me on a deserted river far away.
From a family of brave, upright people,
Gallantry runs in my sage friend in relay.

Lately I met Di, grandson of the minister,
Who lauded you as a "Humanist of the
    Day".
A descendant of a Hanlin Academician
    of an earlier time,
In a minor post of a small county, you
    stay.

You know I got stuck for five days,
By billows on floods coming my way.
A subordinate killed his superior.
By the lake, funeral banners flap in
    display.

I am more depressed alone in a boat.

The route is ultra quiet and faraway.
I was awed by nimble apes and gibbons
    on the side
And above, the enviable vigor of storks
    and cranes in play.

In grief, I should pour wine for myself.
Your help exceeds the courtesy of
    killing a fat sheep that you pay.
Unlike Sima Xiangru, I do not write
    to calm post-war commoners.
I want to rid rebels, like cutting Zhao
    troops of yesterday.

About to go to Chenzhou's calm shores,
I got no words on Changsha's chaos
    right away.
The requested army by Cui Yi has come.
Any mercy from the troops at Li is in
    delay.
If the news of punishing the villains is
    true,
By a lakeside pavilion, I shall smile and
    rest, if I may.

陪斐使君登岳陽樓

湖潤兼雲霧，樓孤屬晚晴。禮加徐孺
子，詩接謝宣城。雪岸叢梅發，春泥
百草生。敢違漁父問，從此更南征。

Climbing Yueyang Tower in the Company of Governor Pei

By a vast lake with cloud and mist,
This lone tower faces late sunset aglow.
As a model of conduct, you excel
　　Xu Ruzi.
Your poems match those of Xie Tiao
　　long ago.
Clumps of plum trees blossom on snowy
　　banks.
In the spring mud, countless herbs grow,
Dare I ignore the answer a fisherman
　　gave Qu Yuan?
Further south from here, on my trip I go.

曉發公安

北城擊柝復欲罷，東方明星亦不遲。
鄰雞野哭如昨日，物色生態能幾時。
舟楫眇然自此去，江湖遠適無前期。
出門轉眄已陳跡，藥餌扶吾隨所之。

Dawn Departure from Gongan

The morning star rises early in the east.
The watch rattle from the north wall
　　stops and starts again.
My neighbor's rooster crows uncurbed
　　like yesterday.
How long can the form and function of
　　nature remain?
I am drifting afar on river and lake.
From here, the sight of my boat in the
　　distance will wane.
My medicine will support me wherever I
　　go.
In a twinkling, to memories my tracks
　　will pertain.

入喬口

漠漠舊京遠，遲遲歸路賒。殘年傍水
國，落日對春華。樹蜜早蜂亂，江泥
輕燕斜。賈生骨已朽，淒惻近長沙。

Entering Qiao Kou

The old capital is blurry and distant.
The plan to return is delayed and hard
　　to follow.
In my waning years, at regions near the
　　waters,
I face spring flowers at sunset.
There is a riot of early bees after the
　　nectar of trees.
Aslant with river mud flies a light
　　swallow.
The bones of Jia Yi have decayed.
Near Changsha, I get depressed and
　　upset.

入衡州

I

兵革自久遠，興衰看帝王。漢儀甚照
耀，胡馬何猖狂。老將一失律，清邊
生戰場。君臣忍瑕垢，河岳空金湯。
重鎮如割據，輕權絕紀綱。軍州體不
一，寬猛性所將。嗟彼苦節士，素於
圓鑿方。寡妻從為郡，兀者安短牆。
凋弊惜邦本，哀矜存事常。旌麾非其
任，府庫實過防。恕己獨在此，多憂
增內傷。偏裨限酒肉，卒伍單衣裳。

II

元惡迷是似，聚謀洩康莊。竟流帳下
血，大降湖南殃。烈火發中夜，高煙
焦上蒼。至今分粟帛，殺氣吹沅湘。
福善理顛倒，明徵天莽茫。銷魂避飛
鏑，累足穿豺狼。隱忍枳棘刺，遷延
胝跰瘡。遠歸兒侍側，猶乳女在旁。
久客幸脫免，暮年慚激昂。蕭條向水

206

陸，泊沒隨魚商。報主身已老，入朝
病見妨。悠悠委薄俗，鬱鬱囘剛腸。

III

參錯走洲渚，春容轉林篁。片帆左郴
岸，通郭前衡陽。華表雲鳥埤，名園
花草香。旗亭壯邑屋，峰櫓蟠城隍。
中有古刺史，盛才冠巖廊。扶顛待柱
石，獨坐飛風霜。昨者問瓊樹，高談
隨羽觴。無論再繾綣，已是安倉黃。
劇孟七國畏，馬卿四賦強。問罪富形
勢，凱歌懸否臧。氛埃期必掃，蚊蚋
焉能當。

IV

橘井舊地宅，仙山引舟航。此行厭暑
雨，厥土聞清涼。諸舅剖符近，開緘
書剳光。頻繁命屢及，磊落字百行。
江總外家養，謝安乘興喪。下流匪珠
玉，擇木羞鸞鳳。我師嵇叔夜，世賢
張子房。柴荊寄樂土，鵬路觀翶翔。

Entering Hengzhou

I

Armed revolts are widespread for long.
Dynastic success or failure relies on the
    king's reign.
The Han order went on very brilliantly.
Why are nomad horsemen so insane?

Once an experienced general fails to
    discipline his troops,
Peaceful frontiers are battlefields again.
The monarch and his ministers bear the
    stain of shame.
River and hill form firm barriers in vain.

Key garrisons are under local control.
Power and law are for warlords to retain.
Military and political systems differ.
From holding the same legal codes, they
    refrain.

I sigh for the governor of Tanzhou.
Like a square peg, in a round hole, he

has lain.
Under him, convicts punished with their
  feet hacked do not grumble.
Widows enjoy the peace his laws help
  maintain.

He feels for commoners of the land in
  ruins.
With empathy, he honors old rules to
  avoid any conflict.
His responsibility rests not with the
  troops.
In guarding the district treasury, he is
  truly too strict.

He is singularly magnanimous on this.
Too much worry increases his mental
  strain.
The lower ranks get limited wine and
  meat.
Only unlined uniforms can soldiers
  obtain.

II

The group plotted their revolt on a big
     road.
To look innocent, the chief culprit could
     feign.
Blood flew by the commander's tent.
A huge disaster fell on Hunan's terrain.

High smoke columns scorched the sky.
A blazing fire started at midnight.
To this day, they still give alms to the
     poor.
A wind of killing rage covered River
     Yuan and Xiang tight.

The logic of "Blessing to Good People"
     is upturned.
This clear Heavenly Commandment is
     masked in oversight.
To escape from flying arrows, I lost my
     wits
And with tired feet, passed through
     jackals and wolves in flight.

Quietly I endured thorns and brambles
And, with calloused limbs, moved from

site to site.
My girl, still nursing, stayed by me with
my son
Who, returning from afar, saw to it I was
alright.

Long a wanderer, I was lucky to have
escaped,
Ashamed to be excitable as my years
were on the wane.
Drearily we went ahead by water and
land,
With the idea of sinking with fishermen
and traders to entertain.

I am already too aged to repay the king.
From going to the court, illnesses force
me to abstain.
Depression catches my upright mind
churning.
About dealing with base customs, on
end I want to complain.

III

Our choice of isles for brisk walks is
   random.
We turn to a bamboo grove with ease
   overall.
By the left bank of Chenzhou, we sail
And head towards Hengyang, past the
   city wall.

Above a grand pillar and parapet, birds
   flit through clouds.
In a famed garden, from blooms to herbs,
   fragrances float.
Banners of pavilions add grandeur to the
   town.
Beacon smoke columns, like masts, coil
   around a city's moat.

The Prefect of Hengzhou is of the old
   style.
To the Hall of Fame as the top honoree,
   his rich talents make him belong.
Propping what teeters needs a pillar
   stone.
He sits apart, with severity like wind,
   frosty and strong.

Recently with the prefect, like an
    alabaster tree,
Over cups of wine, we discuss on and on.
Needless to say, without any further
    friendly gestures,
My panic is already gone.

During the Rebellion of Seven Domains,
    all got awed by Ju Meng.
The four expositions of Sima Xiangru
    read well.
Su Huan made his presence felt with his
    entourage.
In bravery, General Bai Qi could excel.

The situation is ripe for prosecuting
    criminals.
After victory songs comes the judgment
    of good and bad.
I expect a cleanout of evil, like dusty air.
What resistance offenders, like gnats,
    could have had?

IV

I had orange trees by a well at my old
    home.
Drawing my boat now are mountain
    immortals from fairyland.
On this trip, I am tired of heat and rain,
Having heard of the nice, cool weather
    of this land.

An uncle holding a governor's tally is
    nearby.
I open his mail, radiant and splendid.
His frequent letters cover topics on life
    and fate,
 Sharing his views, in a hundred lines,
    clear and candid.

Jiang Zhong was raised by his mother's
    family.
Long did Xie An act differently from the
    mass.
In choosing a branch to perch, I am
    shamed by the white phoenix,
I am no pearl or jade, coming from a
    lower class,

I consider Ji Kang my teacher.
Zhang Zifang is a worthy to any human
    being.
I shall abandon myself to my thatched
    cottage, a happy land,
And watch rocs on their routes take
    wing.

祠南夕望

百丈牽江色，孤舟泛日斜。興來猶扺
屨，目斷更雲沙。山鬼迷春竹，湘娥
倚暮花。湖南清絕地，萬古一長嗟。

Evening View South of the Shrine

Colors of the river spread afar.
My lone boat sails in slanting sunlight.
With a cane and sandals, I am inspired.
Cloud and sand at infinity come in sight.
Mountain spirits get lost among spring
    bamboos.

Xiang ladies lean for flowers at twilight.
I heave a long sigh for the millennia,
South of the lake, at this most serene site.

上水遺懷

I

我衰太平時，身病戎馬後。蹭蹬多拙
為，安得不皓首。驅馳四海內，童稚
日糊口。但遇新少年，少逢舊親友。
低顏下邑地，故人知善誘。後生血氣
豪，舉動見老醜。窮迫挫曩懷，常如
中風走。一紀出西蜀，於今向南斗。
孤舟亂春華，暮齒依蒲柳。冥冥九疑
葬，聖者骨亦朽。

II

蹉跎陶唐人，鞭撻日月久。中間屈賈
輩，讒毀竟自取。鬱悒二悲魂，蕭條

216

猶在否。嶕崒清湘石，逆行雜林藪。
篙工密逞巧，氣若酣杯酒。歌謳互激
遠，回榦明受授。善知應觸類，各藉
穎脫手。古來經濟才，何事獨罕有。
蒼蒼眾色晚，熊掛玄蛇吼。黃羆在樹
顛，正為群虎守。羸骸將何適，履險
顏益厚。庶與達者論，吞聲混瑕垢。

Expressing my Mind as I Go Upstream

I

My health wanes during peacetime.
After wars began, I fell ill.
How can my hair not turn white?
After many inept moves, results are nil.

I rush about in the four seas.
My children are fed barely.
I meet new young people,
But former relatives and friends rarely.

Old friends offer me good advice.

I move around town, never smugly.
Hot-blooded and haughty youngsters
Think my behavior dated and ugly.

Poverty forces me to dwell on the past.
In feverish haste, I usually go.
A dozen years ago, I went to west Shu
And now the Southern Dipper I follow.

In a riot of spring flowers, on a lone boat,
As I age, by rush and willow I stay.
King Shun's tomb at Mount Jiuyi is dark.
Bones of sages suffer decay.

II

Time has been wasted since King Yao.
The sun and the moon have long been
    whipped to roll.
In that interval, the likes of Qu Yuan
    and Jia Yi,
From slander, upon themselves brought
    a toll.

In grief and depression, amid desolation,

Would these two hapless souls still be
　　here?
Tall rugged boulders stand in limpid
　　River Xiang.
Going upstream, past forest and marsh I
　　steer.

Boatmen show their skills often,
With energy from enough brew.
Their songs echo afar,
Warning one another of bends in view.

Good learners should be able to infer.
On wit to handle things well, all rely.
Since early times, why is the talent of
　　management
So singularly rare to come by?

A bear dangles while black snakes roar,
Under a colorful sky at twilight.
A brown grizzly stays at the tree-top.
Tigers in packs watch it tight.

Where will my thin bones be buried?
In danger, my shame becomes less.

I wish to discuss this with someone wise.
Any complaint on faults, I suppress.

登舟將適漢陽

春宅棄汝去，秋帆催客歸。庭蔬尚在
眼，浦浪已吹衣。生理飄蕩拙，有心
遲暮違。中原戎馬盛，遠道素書稀。
塞雁與時集，檣烏終歲飛。鹿門自此
往，永息漢陰機。

Getting on a Boat to Go off to Hanyang

In spring, I give up my house.
By fall, forth on a returning boat I am
   hastened to fare.
Vegetables in my yard are still in sight
When waves have already blown onto
   the robe I wear.

Inept and adrift, I mind my livelihood,

With goals against what an aged man
would care.
War horses are active in the Central
Plain.
From a long way, letters are rare.

Frontier wild geese gather at times.
Crows around masts fly all year.
Henceforth, I shall go to Deer Gate
Mountain,
Forever skipping the schemes of each
socio-political affair.

酬韋韶州見寄

養拙江湖外，朝廷記憶疏。深慚長者
轍，重得故人書。白髮絲難理，新詩
錦不如。雖無南過雁，看取北來魚。

In Answer to a Poem Sent me by Wei of Shaozhou

I nurture my ineptitude beyond river and

lake.
My memories of the palace fade.
I value highly an old friend's letter,
Ashamed of the visit on me you paid.
It is hard to care for my white hair.
Your recent poem overtops brocade.
Though lacking southbound wild geese,
I look for a fish from the north with a
 note you made.

酬郭十五受判官

才微歲老尚虛名，臥病江湖春復生。
藥裹關心詩總廢，花枝照眼句還成。
只同燕石能星隕，自得隋珠覺夜明。
喬口橘洲風浪促，繫帆何惜片時程。

In Answer to Administrative Assistant Guo Shuo, the Fifteenth

Old and sick by river and lake, I face
 another spring.
With hollow fame, I find my talent

slight.

My mind is on my medicine bag, not
poems.

With blooming twigs aglow, I can still
write.

Like stones of Yan, my verses can drop
like meteorites.

I find real worth in yours, like Sui's
pearls that glow at night.

Wind and wave are rough at Qiaokou
and Tangerine Isle.

Moored, why not visit me for a short
respite?

晚秋長沙蔡五侍禦飲筵送殷六參軍歸
澧州覲省

佳士欣相識，慈顏望遠遊。甘從投轄
飲，肯作置書郵。高鳥黃雲暮，寒蟬
碧樹秋。湖南冬不雪，吾病得淹留。

In Late Autumn at Changsha, Censor Cai, the Fifth, Holds a Banquet, Seeing off Military Commander Yin, the Sixth, who is Gong back to Lizhou to See his Parents

As I get to know this fine gentleman,
I learned of his mother looking for him
    far away.
He aims higher than a mail carrier,
Too willing in drinking parties to put
    parting guests in delay.
In fall with cold cicadas and green trees,
Birds fly higher than yellow clouds late
    in the day.
Hunan has no winter snow.
Sick, here I can have a long stay.

北風

北風破南極，朱鳳日威垂。洞庭秋欲
雪，鴻雁將安歸。十年殺氣盛，六合
人煙稀。吾慕漢初老，時清猶茹芝。

224

春生南國瘴，氣待北風蘇。向晚霾殘日，初宵鼓丈鑪。爽攜卑濕地，聲拔洞庭湖。萬里魚龍伏，三更鳥獸呼。滌除貪破浪，愁絕付摧枯。執熱沉沉在，凌寒往往須。且知寬疾肺，不敢恨危途。再宿煩舟子，衰客問僕夫。今晨非盛怒，便道即長驅。隱几看帆席，雲山湧坐隅。

North Wind

A north wind breaks into the extreme
　　south.
Red Phoenix loses its prestige each day.
In fall, it is about to snow at Lake
　　Dongting.
Where will returning wild swans and
　　wild geese stay?

Ten years have passed with massive
　　killings.
All over, human populations are rare.
I admire old hermits of Han on a diet of
　　lingzi in peacetime.

About offered palace jobs, they did not
 care.

Spring lets miasmas rise in the south.
The weather awaits a north wind to
 revive.
Late in the day, with a dark, foggy sky,
Like the bellow of a big furnace, winds
 arrive.

Briskness is brought to low, damp spots.
At Lake Dongting, the pitch reaches its
 height.
On countless miles, fish and dragon hide.
Bird and beast cry out at midnight.

With clarity, I crave a rough voyage.
My dire worries leave me altogether.
Feeling stuck and sunk at heart,
I often need to fight the cold weather.

Further, it would ease my sick lungs.
To resent a dangerous trip, I do not dare.
I trouble the boatman to stay over for a
 second night

And ask the servant about the worn look
  I wear.

This morn, the weather is calm.
We should set out, I say.
By a secluded table, I watch the sails.
As hill-like clouds surge, in a corner seat
  I stay.

湖中送敬十使君適廣陵

相見各頭白，其如離別何。幾年一會
面，今日復悲歌。少壯樂難得，歲寒
心匪他。氣纏霜匣滿，冰置玉壺多。
遭亂突漂泊，濟時曾琢磨。形容吾校
老。膽力爾誰過。秋晚嶽增翠，氣高
湖湧波。騫騰訪知己，淮海莫蹉跎。

On the Lake Seeing off Commissioner Jing, the Tenth, on his Way to Guangling

Separation cannot be helped.
On meeting, our hair is white.
In our reunion after some years,
On this day we sing in a sad plight.

My heart is genuine in the cold season.
In our youth, it was hard to find delight.
Like ice in a jade pot, you are open and
    pure.
The energy fully wrapped around your
    frosty sword case shows fight.

Indeed I wander during wars.
For the state, I have honed my skills to
    do what is right.
I look older than you.
Who can beat you in courage and might?

A tall wind sends billows to the lake.
Fall hills appear greener at night.
Delay not in visiting bosom friends,

Over river and sea, as you take flight.

題衡山縣文宣王廟新學堂呈陸宰

I

旄頭彗紫微，無復俎豆事。金甲相排
蕩，青衿一憔悴。嗚呼已十年，儒服
弊於地。征夫不遑息，學者淪素志。
我行洞庭野，欸得文翁肆。佋佋胄子
行，若舞風雩至。周室宜中興，孔門
未應棄。是以資雅才，煥然立新意。
衡山雖小邑，首唱恢大義。因見縣伊
心，根源舊宮閟。

II

講堂非曩構，大屋加塗墍。下可容百
人，牆隅亦深邃。何必三千徒，始壓
戎馬氣。林木在庭戶，密幹疊蒼翠。
有井朱夏時，轆轤凍階戺。耳聞讀書

229

聲，殺伐災仿佛。故國延歸望，衰顏
減愁思。南紀改波瀾，西河共風味。
采詩倦跋涉，載筆尚可記。高歌激宇
宙，凡百慎失墜。

On the New Study Hall at the Confucius Temple of Mount Heng County, Shown to Magistrate Lu

I

From the nomad banner constellation, a
    comet entered our Purple Tenuity.
In war, the use of ritual vessels was
    suppressed.
Rival soldiers in golden armors clashed.
Civil officials all felt distressed.

O death! It has been ten years.
Confucian costume and code of life have
    left our state.
Soldiers never rest.
The long cherished ambitions of
    scholars disintegrate.

I was in the wilds by Lake Dongting
When suddenly a study hall in the style
　　of Old Wen came in sight.
Many rows of students gathered.
Their chanting resembled dancing in the
　　wind, with a rainbow on site.

Our empire, like that of Zhou, should
　　revive.
Confucianism is not to be thrown away.
We rely on the refined talent in you,
To create and disperse new ideas,
　　making headway.

Though Mount Heng County is small,
To rebuild big morals, it leads the way.
We see in the county magistrate's heart,
With deep-rooted, traditional values as
　　the mainstay.

II

The lecture hall is not the same as
　　before.
The ceiling of this roomy hall has new

plaster on the surface.
Walls from corner to corner run deep.
For a hundred people, there is ample
    space.

Why must there be three thousand
    disciples
Before any curbed thirst for war can be
    seen?
A grove lies by the courtyard door,
With thick, layered trees in dark green.

In torrid summer, there is a well,
With a pulley to get water to chill the
    stairway.
When I hear students reading aloud,
War atrocities seem vague and faraway.

I crave a return to my hometown more
And worry about my waning health less.
Southern waters have different waves.
In style, West River shares the same
    likeness.

Tired of writing poems and traveling on

land and water,
I can still pen my thoughts if I try.
Be really careful not to lose track of
Confucius teachings.
Let me agitate the universe by singing
high.

別蘇徯

故人有遊子，棄擲傍天隅。他日憐才
命，居然屈壯圖。十年猶塌翼，絕倒
為驚呼。消渴今如在，提攜愧老夫。
豈知臺閣舊，先拂鳳凰雛。得實翻蒼
竹，棲枝把翠梧。北辰當宇宙，南嶽
據江湖。國帶風塵色，兵張虎豹符。
數論封內事，揮發府中趨。贈爾秦人
策，莫鞭轅下驅。

Parting from Su Xi

Among my old friends is a wanderer,
Abandoned at the edge of the sky.

Just then I was falling for your talent by
　　fate.
To my surprise, your bold plan gets
　　trashed as time goes by.

After a decade, still with drooping wings,
In admiration, I heave a startled sigh.
Diabetes is still with me.
My shame is the help to you that I have
　　to deny.

How could I know my old associates of
　　the Secretariat
Would first help a chick of the phoenix
　　like you?
Getting your fruit, you will perch on a
　　firmiana branch,
After flying over a gray bamboo.

Polar stars hang high in the universe.
South Mount overlooks river and lake.
This country displays the colors of wind
　　and dust
When, with tiger and leopard tallies, in
　　wars our troops partake.

You will often discuss matters under
  your authority
And deal with issues in the headquarters
  without delay.
Like the man of Qin advising his friend
  on departing,
Do not harass and overwork your young
  workers, I say.

別張十三建封

I

嘗讀唐實錄，國家草昧初。劉裴建首
義，龍見尚躊躇。秦王撥亂姿，一劍
總兵符。汾晉為丰沛，暴隋竟滌除。
宗臣則廟食，後祀何疏蕪。彭城英雄
種，宜膺將相圖。爾唯外曾孫，倜儻
汗血駒。眼中萬少年，用意盡崎嶇。
相逢長沙亭，乍問緒業餘。乃吾故人
子，童丱聯居諸。

揮手灑衰淚，仰看八尺軀。內外名家
流，風神蕩江湖。范雲堪晚友，嵇紹
自不孤。擇材征南牧，潮落囘鯨魚。
載感賈生慟，復聞樂毅書。主憂急盜
賊，師老荒京都。舊丘豈稅駕，大廈
傾宜扶。君臣各有分，管葛本時須。
雖當霰雪嚴，未覺栝柏枯。高義在雲
臺，嘶鳴望天衢。羽人掃碧海，功業
竟何如。

Parting from Zhang Jianfeng, the Thirteenth

I

I have read "Factual Records of the
    Tang Dynasty",
Compiled at the beginning of the state.
Liu and Pei planned the first revolt
When Li Yuan, the Dragon, did hesitate.

Li Shimin, Prince of Qin, led the coup.
His sword pointed to the commander's
    role he could play.
Like Feng-Pui, Fen-Jin area was the site
    of revolution.
At last, the brutal Sui government was
    washed away.

The founding ministers had temples
    with sacrifices,
But how poor later offerings became.
The heroic founding fathers from
    Pengcheng
Should have their portraits in the palace
    Hall of Fame.

You are Liu's great grandson on the
    distaff side,
Like a rare horse, elegant and free.
I see countless other young men
Meet roadblocks in pursuing what they
    want to be

We meet at a pavilion in Changsha.
I first asked of your job, ambition and

more.
You are in fact the son of my old friend.
As a child, you were my neighbor before.

II

I raised my eyes at your great height.
Hand-waving with tears was what this
old man could make.
You have good qualities from both sides
of your family,
With a gallant spirit, over river and lake.

Like FanYun, your loyalty is for life.
Like Ji Shao, you can ask for help from
people you know.
At the southern headquarters, talented
men are being recruited.
Like a whale returning at ebb tide, to
Changsha you should go.

For years I grieve over the death of Jia
Yi.
In a letter, Yue Yi shared with the king
his integrity and insight.

The king is deeply worried about
    bandit-like rebels.
To the capital, outdated armies will
    cause blight.

How can you serve the king if you stay
    in your hometown?
Give your hand if a big house is to fall.
A king and his ministers have different
    duties.
From current needs, Guan Zhong and
    Zhuge Liang answered the call.

Though we face harsh sleet and snow,
I have not seen junipers and cypresses
    decay.
Like Han generals honored at Cloud
    Terrace, you will be in history.
You should ride your neighing horse on
    the imperial highway.

In success, like a feathered immortal
    sweeping the emerald sea,
What will your achievements be?

過洞庭湖

蛟室圍青草，龍堆隱白沙。護堤盤古
木，迎櫂舞神鴉。破浪南風正，回檣
畏日斜。湖光與天遠，直欲泛仙槎。

Passing over Lake Dongting

Green grass circles the chamber of flood
  dragons.
At White Sands Isle, dragon piles are
  not clear.
Old trees coil to guard the embankment.
To direct the oars, dancing sacred crows
  appear.
In the direct, wave-breaking south wind,
We turn the mast to avert sunset and our
  fear.
I watch the simmering lake and far sky,
Hoping for a ride on the Fairy Raft that
  is held dear.

過南嶽入洞庭湖

洪波忽爭道，岸轉異江湖。鄂渚分雲
樹，衡山引舳艫。翠芽穿裹蔣，碧節
上寒浦。病渴身何去，春生力更無。

Past the Southern Great Mountain, into Lake Dongting

A different bank has a new waterscape.
Sudden huge waves vie for a course in
the flow.
By Mount Heng, my rectangular boat
moves on.
On E Isle, trees among clouds clearly
show.
Green nodes of reeds push up in the cold.
Through wild rice stems, jade-like
sprouts grow.
Spring is here, but I feel weak.
Sick and thirsty, where shall I go?

清明

著處繁花矜是日，長沙千人萬人出。
渡頭翠柳艷明眉，爭道朱蹄驕齧膝。
此都好遊湘西寺，諸將亦自軍中至。
馬援征行在眼前，葛強親近同心事。

Qingming Festival

Everywhere dense blooms brag today.
Countless Changsha people come out to
    play.
At the ford with green willows are ladies
    with charming, bright brows.
Some red-hoofed, knee-biting horses
    proudly fight for the roadway.
A visit to Xiangxi Temple is where
    locals like to pay.
To reach here, generals also make way.
A subordinate, like Ge Qiang, likes to
    join the commoners.
The commander, like Ma Yuan, will
    lead an expedition right away.

公安縣懷古

野曠呂蒙營，江深劉備城。寒天催日短，風浪與雲平。灑落君臣契，飛騰戰伐名。維舟倚前浦，長嘯一含情。

Recalling the Past at Gongan

By a deep river in the wide wilderness,
Gongan, in Liu Bei's reign, was Lu
    Meng's campsite.
In the cold, daylight hours are short.
Windswept waves reach the clouds'
    height.
Liu Bei and Zhuge Liang reached a
    war strategy easily.
Lu Meng's famous army flew in action
    with might.
As I moor by the shore ahead,
I let out a loud whistle with emotion on
    site.

奉贈李八丈判官曛

I

我丈時英特，宗枝神堯後。珊瑚市則
無，騄驥人得有。早年見標格，秀氣
衝星斗。事業富清機，官曹正獨守。
傾來樹嘉政，皆已傳泉口。艱難禮貴
安，冗長吾敢取。區區猶歷試，炯炯
更持久。討論實解頤，操割紛應手。

II

筐書積諷諫，宮闕限奔走。入幕未展
材，秉鈞孰為偶。所親問淹泊，泛愛
惜衰朽。垂白亂南翁，委身希北叟。
真成窮轍鮒，或似喪家狗。秋枯洞庭
石，風颯長沙柳。高興激荊衡，知音
為回首。

Respectfully Presented to Magistrate Li Xun, the Eighth

I

Sir, you are exceptional in these times,
A descendant of "Holy Yao", from the
    royal family tree.
Who among us can be a rare horse?
For sale in markets, corals are not meant
    to be.

Your refined manners shine forth like
    constellations.
You were exemplary in an early year,
Upholding integrity singularly in
    Officialdom,
You are organized in your career.

Of late, you practice good management,
Something already passed on and talked
    about.
In hardship, people value safety and
    politeness.
Who needs rules that are tedious and

long-drawn-out?

Still being tested in a minor post,
Brilliantly you persevere.
You resolve all problems smoothly
And to discussions, bring cheer.

II

Admonitions to the emperor pile up in
  your chest of books.
In governance, who is your peer?
In the headquarters, you fail to develop
  your talent
And to the palace, cannot get near.

Those kind to me ask of my wanderings.
The overall concern is on my health in
  decay.
Upset and white-haired, I am heading
  south.
To be a frontier warrior in the north, I
  pray.

Truly I have become a carp stuck in

carriage ruts
Or a dog that has lost its home.
Winds rustle through the willows of
　Changsha.
Rocks of Lake Dongting age when
　autumn days come.

At Jingzhou, under Mount Heng, I feel
　touched in glee,
For the special regard my bosom friends
　give me.

送覃二判官

先帝弓劍遠，小臣餘此生。蹉跎病江
漢，不復謁承明。餞爾白頭日，永懷
丹鳳城。遲遲戀屈宋，渺渺臥荊衡。
魂斷航舸失，天寒沙水清。肺肝若稍
愈，亦上赤霄行。

Seeing off Magistrate Tan, the Second

The former king's tomb is afar.
As a minor official for life, I remain.
By Yangzi and Han, I idle being sick,
Unable to pay respects at Chengming
    Palace again.

At your farewell feast, white-haired,
The memory of Changan, I will forever
    retain.
With my lasting memory for Qu Yuan
    and Song Yu,
At Jing and Heng, as an unknown I have
    lain.

Sand and water are clear under a cold
    sky,
With me broken-hearted as images of
    your boat wane.
Let me present a ballad of the court
If the health of my lungs and liver has
    a slight gain.

發劉郎浦

挂帆早發劉郎浦，疾風颯颯昏亭午。
舟中無日不沙塵，岸上空村盡豺虎。
十日北風風未廻，客行歲晚晚相催。
白頭厭伴漁人宿，黃帽青鞋歸去來。

Setting out from Master Liu's Shore

We set sail from Master Liu's Shore
    early in the day,
With a swift, whistling wind and dark
    sky by midday.
The boat is dusty the whole time.
By deserted villages ashore, only jackals
    and tigers stay.
The north wind blowing for ten days has
    not turned around.
I feel hurried at the year's end as my trip
    just got off the ground.
White haired, I am tired of spending
    nights among fishermen.
With a yellow hat and green sandals, I
    am homeward bound.

發潭州

夜醉長沙酒，曉行湘水春。岸花飛送客，檣燕語留人。賈傅才未有，褚公書絕倫。高名前後事，回首一傷神。

Setting out from Tanzhou

I get drunk at night on Changsha wine,
Sailing at dawn on River Xiang on a
spring day.
Flying petals from the shore see me off.
Swallows by the mast ask me to stay.
Banished to Tanzhou was Jia Yi, a
talented tutor,
And Chu Suiliang, a top calligrapher of
yesterday.
With great fame, they suffered at
different times.
On looking back, I feel depressed in the
same way.

登白馬潭

水生春纜沒，日出野船開。宿鳥行猶
去，叢花笑不來。人人傷白首，處處
接金杯。莫道新知要，南征且未回。

Setting out from White Horse Pool

The rising water hides the anchor ropes
   in spring.
My boat in the wilds sets out at sunrise.
Clumps of open flowers are out of reach.
In lines, overnight birds fly to the skies.
Everyone laments over white hair.
Everywhere golden goblets of wine I get.
Do not say new friends will invite me.
From my southbound trip, I have not
   been back yet.

湘夫人祠

蕭蕭湘妃廟，空牆碧水春。蟲書玉佩
蘚，燕舞翠帷塵。晚泊登汀樹，微馨
借渚蘋。蒼梧恨不盡，染淚在叢筠。

The Shrine of the Ladies of the Xiang

A solemn temple of the Ladies of River
    Xiang stands
With bare walls, as spring green waters
    flow.
Like jade pendants, insects on moss
    make calligraphy.
In the dust of kingfisher drapes is a
    dancing swallow.
I go ashore at night, after mooring by a
    tree.
From duckweeds of a sandbar, a slight
    fragrance is lent.
Still on bamboo clumps are tear stains
    of the ladies,
Over the king's death at Cangwu, with
    endless lament.

醉歌行贈公安顏少府請顧八題壁

神仙中人不易得，顏氏之子才孤標。
天馬長鳴待駕馭，秋鷹整翮當雲霄。
君不見　東吳顧文學？
君不見　西漢杜陵老？
詩家筆勢君不嫌，詞翰升堂為君掃。

是日霜風凍七澤，烏蠻落照銜赤壁。
酒酣耳熱忘頭白，感君意氣無所惜，
一為歌行歌主客。

Song Written while Drunk, a Ballad Presented to Sheriff Yan of Gongan, after Asking Gu, the Eighth, to Write it on the Wall

It is not easy to see another future fairy
   like you,
A talented son of Yan and the only
   model for all.
You are Heaven's neighing steed to be
   engaged
Or among clouds, a preening eagle of

fall.

Sir, have you not seen
Gu, a literary man, like Scholar Gu of
   East Wu?
Sir, have you not seen
Me, an old man, from Duling clan since
   West Han?
If you do not mind my poetic flair,
My verse in his brush calligraphy and
   strokes enters your hall.

On Red Cliff near Qiang nomads, sunset
   is everywhere.
A frosty wind today chills seven
   marshes.
Fully wined, I forgot about my gray hair.
I chant this ballad for both the host and
   guests.
Moved by your energy, my heart I bare.

宿白沙驛

水宿仍餘照，人煙復此亭。驛邊沙舊
白，湖外草新青。萬象皆春氣，孤槎
自客星。隨波無限月，的的近南溟。

Staying over at White Sands Post Station

Lodging by waters, I still find the last
    sunshine.
From this station, people and their
    cooking smoke are again seen.
Sands are white as before at the edge.
Beyond the lake, new grass looks green.
I am a wanderer for the stars from a
    lone raft.
Myriad images here are spring-like and
    serene.
My boat follows waves for the dark
    South Sea,
Under endless moonlight with a sheen.

宿鑿石浦

早宿賓從勞，仲春江山麗。飄風過無
時，舟楫敢不繫。囘塘澹暮色，日沒
眾星嘒。缺月殊未生，青燈死分翳。
窮途多俊異，亂世少恩惠。鄙夫亦放
蕩，草草頻卒歲。斯文憂患餘，聖哲
垂象繫。

Staying Overnight at Rock Quarry Shore

In mid-spring, river and hill look lovely.
The crew has worked hard; we retire
   early for the night.
A gust may come anytime.
We dare not skip tying up the boat tight.

At sunset, stars are small and faint.
The winding pool looks pale at twilight.
My waning blue lamp comes in and out.
The moon is nowhere in sight.

I find little kindness in an age of turmoil.

Many at life's dead-ends are very bright.
A humble man like me, as a wanderer,
Often fails to celebrate New Year's Eve
    properly from oversight.
Intellectuals are too worried.
In "Appended Remarks" are words of
    sages on what is morally right.

早行

歌哭俱在曉，行邁有期程。孤舟似昨
日，聞見同一聲。飛鳥數求食，潛魚
亦獨驚。前王作網罟，設法害生成。
碧藻非不茂，高帆終日征。干戈未揖
讓，崩迫開其情。

Traveling Early

A far journey has its schedule.
I chant and weep at the break of day.
Hearing the same sounds on board,
I find the lone boat no different from

yesterday.

A submerged fish is in fright by itself.
Several birds seek food in relay.
Former kings set nets for entrapment,
With schemes to harm the living in play.

All day, my boat with tall sails move on.
Green seaweeds are not in decay.
Forced to flee, I open up my mind
Since wars are still going to stay.

過楝

I

宿昔世安命，自私猶畏天。勞生繫一
物，為客費多年。衡嶽江湖大，蒸池
疫癘偏。散才嬰薄俗，有跡負前賢。
巾拂那關眼，瓶罍易滿船。火雲滋垢
膩，凍雨裹沉綿。強飯蓴添滑，端居
茗續煎。清思漢水上，涼憶峴山巔。

順浪翻堪倚，迴帆又省牽，五家碑不
昧，王氏井依然。几杖將衰齒，茅茨
寄短椽。灌園曾取適，遊寺可終焉。
遂性同漁夫，成名異魯連。篙師煩爾
送，朱夏及寒泉。

Turning my Boat

I

Selfish people are in awe of Heaven.
To fate, they are used to resign.
I labor all my life with almost nothing.
For years, a wanderer's life is mine.

River and lake by Mount Heng are huge.
To steamy ponds, miasmas confine.
My track lags behind those of past sages.
Weak in talent, with base local customs
    I align.

Turban and duster do not catch my eyes.

My boat has easily full crocks of wine.
Oily or grimy and damp or wet,
I live, fiery or chilly and rain or shine.

This is proper living with endless tea-
    boiling.
On tender water-shields and rice, I force
    myself to dine.
For River Han and Mount Xian,
Clearly and coolly, I pine.

II

Turning my boat saves towing.
Relying on the wind, with currents I am
    in line.
My ancestral stele is not hidden.
The Wang family well still looks fine.

I will live in a thatched hut with short
    beams.
In waning health, with a cane by a table
    I recline.
I have found it fit to water my garden.
Visiting temples in future I can decline.

My fame will differ from Lu Zhonglian,
    the persuader.
To be a fisherman, by nature I am
    inclined.
Boatman, let me trouble you to take me
To where red-hot summers and cold
    springs can be combined.

樓上

天地空搔首，頻抽白玉簪。皇輿三極
北，身事五湖南。 戀闕勞肝肺，論才
愧杞楠。亂離難自救，終是老湘潭。

Upstairs in the Tower

Often reattaching my white jade hairpin,
Between Heaven and Earth, I scratch my
    head in vain.
The imperial coach is north of the Three
    Poles.
South of the Five Lakes, an interest to

serve the state I sustain.
I feel shamed of my talents before
    intellectual giants.
Yearnings for the palace give me stress
    and strain.
It is hard to save myself in war and
    displacement.
In Xiangtan, I shall age and wane.

冬深

花葉隨天意，江溪共石根。早霞隨類
影，寒水各依痕。易下楊朱淚，難招
楚客魂。風濤暮不穩，捨棹宿誰門。

Well into Winter

River and brook come from the same
    rocky base.
Heaven's will is what flower and leaf
    follow.
In cold weather, waters flow along the
    same watermark.

Each dawn cloud has its unique shadow.
Like Qu Yuan, my soul will not be
easily summoned.
Like Yang Zhu, I readily shed my tears
of sorrow.
Wind and wave do not calm down at
twilight.
Ashore for overnight, to which door can
I go?

小寒食舟中作

佳辰強飲食猶寒，隱几蕭條戴鶡冠。
春水如雨天上坐，老年花似霧中看。
娟娟戲蝶過閒幔，片片輕鷗下急湍。
雲白山青萬餘里，愁看直北是長安。

Written on a Boat during the Minor Cold Festival

At this fine hour, with food still cold,
I force myself to drink alright.
In a hermit's cap, by the table alone I

sit tight.

My boat on spring waters seems to float
in the sky.

Blooms appear misty, to an old man's
sight.

Pretty, playful butterflies fly past still
drapes.

Over the rapids, gulls are light-bodied in
flight.

In grief, I watch for Changan in the far
north.

For endless miles, above green hills,
clouds look bright.

2. POEMS NOT IN CHRONOLOGY

夜宿西閣曉呈元二十一曹長

城暗更籌急，樓高雨雪微。稍通綃幕
霽，遠帶玉繩稀。門鵲晨光起，檣鳥
宿處飛。寒江流甚細，有意待人歸。

After Spending the Night at West Pavilion, I Present this Verse at Dawn to Bureau Chief Yuan, the Twenty-first

At the dark city wall, watch rattles
  sound tight,
With slight icy rain on the tower at a
  height.
Through silk drapes passes rare sunlight.
Afar, vaguely the constellation "Jade
  Rope" comes in sight.
In dawn light, magpies from the gate
  take flight.
Crows by the mast fly from where they
  stayed overnight.

The cold river seems quite sluggish,
Wishing to wait for my trip home from
  this site.

季夏送鄉弟韶陪黃門從叔朝謁

令弟尚為蒼水使，名家莫出杜陵人。
比來相國兼安蜀，歸赴朝廷已入秦。
舍舟策馬論兵地，拖玉腰金報主身。
莫度清秋吟蟋蟀，早聞黃閣畫麒麟。

**At the End of Summer, Seeing off my
Younger Clansman, Shao, who will
Accompany my Cousin-uncle of the
Chancellery, to Pay Respects to the
Court**

My fine younger clansman is another
  "Blue Waters Emissary".
The same honor that Duling families get
  no others can claim.
For a return to the court at Changan,
As an envoy to Shu, the minister now

266

came.
After mooring, you gallop off near
battlefields.
Decked out in jade and gold, you report
to the king in your name.
Do not pass clear fall days chanting on
crickets.
In the palace, we have heard of portraits
of honorees in the Hall of Fame.

銅瓶

亂後碧井廢，時清瑤殿深。銅瓶未失
水，百丈有哀音。側想美人意，應悲
寒蕊沈。蛟龍半缺落，猶得折黃金。

Bronze Pitcher

In peaceful times, it is deep within the
palace.
The jade well is abandoned after wars
unfold.
From a great depth come sad sounds.

There is water that a bronze pitcher can
    hold.
I think hard how the beauty felt.
It must be grief in drowning within
    walls so cold.
Carved flood dragons, though half
    broken,
May still bring in some stacks of gold.

柳邊

只道梅花發，那知柳亦新。枝枝總到
地，葉葉自開春。紫燕時翻翼，黃鸝
不露身。漢南應老盡，霸上遠愁人。

By the Willows

They talk of plum trees blossoming.
About new looks of willows, who would
    know?
Their leaves have opened in spring.
To the ground, all willow branches grow.
Purple swallows do somersaults at times.

Bodies of yellow orioles do not show.
I should age in South of the River.
Afar by River Ba, people part with
willow twigs in sorrow.

上牛頭寺

青山意不盡，衰衰上牛頭。無復能拘
礙，真成浪出遊。花濃春寺靜，竹細
野池幽。何處鶯啼切，移時獨未休。

Climbing to Oxhead Temple

I persist and climb to Oxhead Temple,
In my endless zest for the green hill.
No more do I feel restricted,
On this truly carefree trip to my will.
The nameless pool is quiet with slim
bamboos.
With dense spring flowers, the temple is
still.
In time, one birdsong never rests.
Where comes this oriole's piercing trill?

寒食

寒食江村路，風花高下飛。汀煙輕冉冉，竹日淨暉暉。田父要皆去，鄰家問不違。地偏相識盡，雞犬亦忘歸。

Cold Food Festival

Near the Cold Food Festival, on village
    roads by the river,
Flowers drop in the wind from a height.
Light mists by the shore gradually rise.
Clean and straight bamboos bask in
    sunlight.
I accept requests from all farmers to
    drink.
With invitations from neighbors, I never
    put up a fight.
Even chickens and dogs forget to return
When in this remote place, I know
    everyone by sight.

槐葉冷淘

青青高槐葉，采掇付中廚。新麵來近
市，汁滓宛相俱。入鼎資過熟，加餐
愁欲無。碧鮮俱照箸，香飯兼苞蘆。
經齒冷於雪，勸人投比珠。願隨金騕
褭，走置錦屠蘇。路遠思恐泥，興深
終不渝。獻芹則小小，薦藻明區區。
萬里露寒殿，開冰清玉壺。君王納涼
晚，此味亦時須。

Cold Wet Noodle Dish with Leaves of the Locust Tree

I send green leaves to the kitchen,
After plucking them from a locust tree
　　at a height.
Fresh noodles from a nearby market
Get mixed with the juice and shreds just
　　right.
The food is cooked in a pot.
I eat more, worrying it may be out of
　　sight.
The fragrant rice comes with reed shoots.

On my chopsticks, the jade green sheen
    looks bright.
Past my teeth, it feels colder than snow.
That it is like pearls, to urge others I say.
I wish to rush it to a fine lodge like
    brocade,
On a golden charger, like Yao Niao, on
    my way.
The far road may be boggy,
But my deep interest holds sway.
To present celeries may be trivial.
Offering this shows clearly the respect I
    pay.
Add ice to a pot like translucent jade,
In Cold Dew Palace, countless miles
    away.
This delicacy is needed at that moment
When the king enjoys the cool, at the
    end of the day.

通泉驛南去通泉縣十五里山水作

溪行衣自濕，亭午氣始散。冬溫蚊蚋在，人遠鳧鴨亂。登頓生曾陰，欹傾出高岸。驛樓衰柳側，縣郭輕煙畔。一川何綺麗，盡目窮壯觀。山色遠寂寞，江光夕滋蔓。傷時愧孔父，去國同王粲。我生苦飄零，所歷有嗟嘆。

Composed in the Landscape, Fifteen Miles Going South from Tongquan Post Station to Tongquan County

Only at noon does the humidity leave.
A walk along the creek gets our clothes
   wet.
Ducks spread out at random, if far from
   people.
In warm winter, flies and gnats are not
   gone yet.

Stooping aslant, I leave a high bank.
In climbing and halting, we watch
   layers of shadows.

The county seat is near light mists.
Beside the station stand waning willows.

How pretty is the stream!
For the grand vista, I strain my eyes.
The mountain scene is distant and quiet.
The evening shimmer of the river
    multiplies.

I am ashamed for failing Confucius in
    our national crisis.
Like Wang Can, I left the country for a
    barbarian land.
Spending my life as a wanderer in pain,
I sigh over my experience first-hand.

承聞故房相公靈櫬自閬州啓殯歸葬東
都有作二首，其一

遠聞房太尉，歸葬陸渾山。一德興王
後，孤魂久客閒。孔明多故事，安石
竟崇班。他日嘉陵涕，仍霑楚水還。

Composed when I Heard that the Casket of the Former Minister Fang had been Taken from its Temporary Resting Place in Langzhou and Returned to the East Capital for Burial, no.1

Commander-in-chief Fang is back
To be buried at Luhun Hill, from afar I
  learn.
After restoring the monarchy, a virtuous
  act,
His lone soul was long put away, with
  no concern.
Kong Ming left many historical
  anecdotes.
Wang Anshi got an exalted rank that he
  did not earn.
In future, my tears by River Jialing
Will again wet Chu's river on my return.

承聞故房相公靈櫬自閬州啓殯歸葬東都有作二首，其二

浩浩終不息，乃知東極臨。眾流歸海意，萬國奉君心。色借瀟湘潤，聲驅灩澦深。未辭添霧雨，接上遇衣襟。

Composed when I Heard that the Casket of the Former Minister Fang had been Taken from its Temporary Resting Place in Langzhou and Returned to the East Capital for Burial, no.2

I know of the end of the eastward flow
When vast bodies of water do not wane.
All rivulets want to join to reach the sea,
Like the consent to serve the king from
    each domain.
The broad rivers, Xiao and Xiang, lend
    their colors.
Beyond the depths by Yanyu Rocks, the
    sound cannot sustain.
The lapels of my robe will get wet
If I do not mind the extra fog and rain.

促織

促織甚微細，哀音何動人。草根吟不
穩，床下意相親。久客得無淚，放妻
難及晨。悲絲與急管，感激異天真。

Crickets

Crickets are very tiny.
How moving are their sounds in sorrow!
At the grassroots, their chirping is not
　　steady.
Under a bed, they offer intensity from
　　below.
Can a long-term wanderer be tearless?
Through the night, a spurned queen was
　　in woe.
Sad strings and shrill pipes move us
　　differently
Than what real notes in nature can go.

暝

日下四山陰，山庭嵐氣侵。牛羊歸徑
險，鳥雀聚枝深。正枕當星劍，收書
動玉琴。半扉開燭影，欲掩見清砧。

Darkness

All hills look dark at the end of the day.
On a hillside courtyard, mists intrude
    as an overlay.
Cattle and sheep return on steep trails.
Deep in trees, birds gather to stay.
I straighten my pillow before my sword
    with stars
And strike my jade zither after putting
    my books away.
Candlelight escapes through my gate
    half ajar,
Showing clear mallets before I close the
    entryway.

久客

羈旅知交態，淹留見俗情。衰顏聊自
哂，小吏最相輕。去國哀王粲，傷時
哭賈生。狐狸何足道，豺虎正縱橫。

A Detained Wanderer

A detained wanderer knows about
    human relationships.
After long stays, I have seen customs
    and habits at each site.
I put myself down for my aging look.
Minor clerks give me the biggest slight.
Wang Can grieved over leaving his
    country.
Jia Yi wept over how bad the state was
    run.
Petty people, like foxes, can be ignored.
By rebels, like jackals and tigers, our
    empire is overrun.

雙楓浦

輟棹雙楓浦，雙楓舊已催。自驚衰謝
力，不道棟梁材。浪足浮紗帽，皮須
截錦苔。江邊地有主，暫借上天廻。

Double Maple Strand

We moor at Double Maple Strand
Where two maples, old and decayed,
   lie.
My waning strength gives me fright.
Any claim of top talent I deny.
I need to clean the bark of moss like
   brocade.
Waves that can let a gauze hat float are
   not high.
If this place by the river has an owner,
Let me borrow the lumber for my raft
   to the sky.

九日五首，其一

重陽獨酌杯中酒，抱病豈登江上臺。
竹葉於人既無分，菊花從此不須開。
殊方日落玄猿苦，舊國霜前白雁來。
弟妹蕭條各何往，干戈衰謝兩相催。

The Double Ninth Day, no.1

How can a sick man climb a riverside
    terrace?
On the Double Ninth day, I drink my
    cup of wine alone.
Let chrysanthemums end blooming from
    now on.
For liking bamboo leaf brew, I am not
    known.
At sunset on a strange land, black
    gibbons weep.
Before the frost, white wild geese from
    my hometown have flown.
Besides the pressure of wars and my
    waning health,
The whereabouts of my forlorn siblings
    cannot be shown.

九日五首，其二

舊日重陽日，傳杯不放杯。即今蓬鬢
改，但愧菊花開。北闕心長戀，西江
首獨回。茱萸賜朝士，難得一枝來。

The Double Ninth Day, no.2

We passed wine cups without rest,
Formerly on the Double Ninth Day.
Blooming chrysanthemums shame me
When my disheveled hair has changed
   its color today.
Alone on West River, I head back,
But my yearnings for the northern
   palace always stay.
Twigs of prickly ash are bestowed on
   court officials.
It is hard to see one coming my way.

獨酌

步屧深林晚，開樽獨酌遲。仰蜂黏落
絮，行蟻上枯梨。薄劣慚真隱，幽偏
得自怡。本無軒冕意，不是傲當時。

Drinking Wine Alone

I walk deep in the woods late in the day,
With plans to drink wine alone in delay.
A bee flying up sticks to falling fluff.
Ants in line climb a pear tree in decay.

True hermits put an inferior man like me
    to shame.
I just enjoy seclusion in my own way.
With no intention to scorn the present
    elite,
In my mind, thoughts for high office
    never stay.

解憂

減米散同舟，　路難思共濟。向來雲濤
盤，　眾力亦不細。呀坑瞥眼過，　飛櫓
本無蔕。得失瞬息閒，　致遠宜恐泥。
百慮視安危，　分明襄賢計。茲理庶可
廣，　拳拳期勿替。

Easing my Worries

The rice I cut back is divided among
    others on the boat.
The route is hard and I think of the need
    to be interdependent.
Cloud-like waves swirl all day.
Not miniscule are the many hands lent.

Flying oars are not tied down.
In the blink of an eye, gaping gullies
    came and went.
To reach afar, we should fear being
    bogged down.
Success or failure hangs on a quick
    moment.

In planning, the major concern is safety.
That worthies of old embraced it is
    evident.
This line of reasoning can be expanded.
I earnestly hope against a replacement.

十六夜玩月

舊挹金波爽，皆傳玉露秋。關山隨地
潤，河漢近人流。谷口樵歸唱，孤城
笛起愁。巴童渾不寢，半夜有行舟。

Enjoying the Moon on the Sixteenth

They used to scoop up moonlit waves,
    golden and fresh,
As jade dew in fall, according to hearsay.
Wide passes and hills are everywhere,
Near me flows the Milky Way.
Woodcutters sing at the mouth of the
    valley.
In the lonesome town, sad flute notes are

in play.
All lads of Ba do not sleep at midnight,
Rowing their boats to get away.

玩月呈漢中王

夜深露氣清，江月滿江城。浮客轉危
坐，歸舟應獨行。關山同一照，烏鵲
自多驚。欲得淮王術，風吹暈已身。

Enjoying the Moon, Presented to Prince of Hanzhong

Deep into the night, with clear dewy air,
The moonlit, riverside town is all aglow.
On a boat, you must be returning alone.
A drifter slowly sitting upright lets his
    wariness show.
Without a patron, I am a lone magpie
    in constant fright.
To passes and hills, the same beams of
    moonlight go.
I wish to get the book on governance by

the king of Huainan.
In the wind, there is already a lunar halo.

夜

絕岸風威動，寒房燭影微。嶺猿霜外
宿，江鳥夜深飛。獨坐親雄劍，哀歌
嘆短衣。煙塵繞閭闔，白首壯心違。

Evening

The remote bank shakes under the
wind's might.
In my cold room, the candle flame is
slight.
Gibbons of the ridges stay beyond the
frost.
Riverside birds fly deep into the night.
I sit alone by my sword like a male
dragon.
My commoner status makes me chant in
a sad plight.
To a white-haired man with ambitions

gone,
Smoke and dust of war near the palace
still come in sight.

遣悶戲呈路十九曹長

江浦雷聲喧昨夜，　春城雨色動微寒。
黃鸝並坐交愁濕，　白鷺群飛大劇乾。
晚節漸於詩律細，　誰家數去酒杯寬。
唯君最愛清狂客，　百遍相遇意未闌。

Expressing my Boredom, Playfully Shown to Vice-director Lu, the Nineteenth

Spring rain in the city evokes slight chill,
With a loud thunder above the riverbank
last night.
Yellow orioles, side by side, worry
about dampness.
To dry up fast, white egrets in groups
take flight.
Old, I tend to mind detailed rules of

prosody.
To whose house do I often go for free wine?
Your most savored guest is mildly mad.
He visits you a hundred times and your interest does not decline.

遣興廿三首，其一

朔風飄胡雁，慘澹帶砂礫。長林何蕭蕭，秋草萋更碧。北里富薰天，高樓夜吹笛。焉知南鄰客，九月猶絺綌。

Expressing my Inspiration in Twenty-three Poems, no.1

A north wind tosses nomad wild geese,
With pebbles and sand, in a cheerless flight.
In fall, lush grasses look greener.
How hard winds whistle through a tall forest!
In the north, wealth overwhelms the sky,

With flutists in high towers playing at
    night.
How would they know their southern
    neighbors, in the ninth month,
In coarse homespun, are still dressed?

遣興廿三首，其二

長陵銳頭兒，出獵待明發。駢弓金爪
鏑，白馬蹴微雪。未知所馳逐，但見
暮光減。歸來懸兩狼，門戶有旌節。

Expressing my Inspiration in Twenty-three Poems, no.2

A smart, tough man of Changling
Sets out to hunt in dawn light,
With red bows and golden claw
    arrowheads.
Snow kicked up by his white horse is
    slight.
I know not what he is after,
But see him return in fading twilight.

He has two wolves hung on his horse.
His gate has flag and staff for high
    officials on site.

遣興廿三首，其三

漆有用而割，膏以明自煎。蘭摧白露
下，桂折秋風前。府中羅舊尹，沙道
尚依然。赫赫蕭京北，今為時所憐。

Expressing my Inspiration in Twenty-three Poems, no.3

The lacquer tree is cut for use.
Oil burns up for brightness cast.
Orchids get wrecked under white dew.
Cassias snap under a fall blast.
From the office, they caught the former
    governor.
Still the sandy path to his mansion did
    last.
Xiao of the capital, once prominent,
Is now pitied as an outcast.

遣興廿三首，其四

猛虎憑其威，往往遭急縛。雷吼徒咆
哮，枝撐已在腳。忽看皮寢處，無復
睛閃爍。人有甚於斯，足以勸無惡。

Expressing my Inspiration in Twenty-three Poems, no.4

The fierce tiger, relying on its menacing
    stance,
Can get bound rapidly, time and again.
Wooden braces are already on its paws,
Leaving his thunderous roars in vain.
The flash of its pupils is no more
When you see how on its pelt bedding it
    has lain.
This is enough to warn the most wicked.
Worse results are what they may gain.

遣興廿三首，其五

朝逢富家葬，前後皆輝光。共指親戚
大，緦麻百夫行。送者各有死，不須
羨其強。君看束縛去，亦得歸山崗。

Expressing my Inspiration in Twenty-three Poems, no.5

The whole funeral cortege was gorgeous
That at dawn I met from the well-to-do.
All noted the magnitude of relatives,
In fine mourning attire, about a hundred
   in queue.
Those attending will die eventually.
Any envious feeling is undue.
Sir, also going to the burial mounds
Are those barely tied and wrapped, in
   plain view.

遣興廿三首，其六

蟄龍三冬臥，老鶴萬里心。昔時賢俊
人，未遇猶視今。嵇康不得死，孔明
有知音。又如壟底松，用舍在所尋。
大哉霜雪幹，歲久為枯林。

Expressing my Inspiration in Twenty-three Poems, no.6

An old crane sets its mind to cover
    endless miles.
All winter, a hibernating dragon lies.
Now as in the past, those missing their
    chances
May well be the worthy and wise.
Ji Kang met his unfitting death.
With friends of like minds, Kong Ming
    made ties.
It is also like the pine below a mound
Which is sought for use or otherwise.
Big indeed is the trunk under frost and
    snow
That in time, as part of the wilted grove,
    dies.

遣興廿三首，其七

昔者龐德公，未曾入州府。襄陽耆老
聞，處士節獨苦。豈無濟時策，終竟
畏羅罟。林茂鳥有歸，水深魚知聚。
舉家隱鹿門，劉表焉得取。

Expressing my Inspiration in Twenty-three Poems, no.7

One who refused a government post
Was Pang Degong of a yesteryear.
Among the seniors of Xiangyang,
This recluse stuck to beliefs held dear.
Surely he had plans to heal current
    troubles,
But in the end, political nets and snares
    made him fear.
Birds return to dense forests.
In deep waters, fish in schools appear.
How could Liu Biao recruit him?
To a hermit's life at Deergate, the
    whole family wanted to adhere.

遣興廿三首，其八

陶潛避俗翁，未必能達道。觀其著詩集，頗亦恨枯槁。達生豈是足，默識蓋不早。有子賢與愚，何其掛懷抱。

Expressing my Inspiration in Twenty-three Poems, no.8

Tao Qian who avoided social contacts
Might not be a true Daoist yet.
As I read his collected poems,
I find his life dull, to my regret.
His mind was early closed to intuition.
In his way, the goal of a fulfilled life is
    unmet.
Sons may be wise or stupid.
Why should one keep getting upset?

遣興廿三首，其九

賀公雅吳語，在位常清狂。上疏乞骸
骨，黃冠歸故鄉。爽氣不可致，斯人
今則亡。山陰一茅宇，江海日淒涼。

Expressing my Inspiration in Twenty-three Poems, no.9

Mister He handled the Wu dialect with
　　grace,
Acting mildly mad on duty, in his way.
With a yellow hat, he returned home
On a petition for his bones after death,
　　in his hometown, to stay.
His clear-cut temperament has no match.
This man has perished today.
In a thatched cottage, south of the hills,
By river and sea, I am sadder each day.

遣興廿三首，其十

吾憐孟浩然，短褐即長夜。賦詩何必
多，往往凌鮑謝。清江空舊魚，春雨
餘甘蔗。每望東南雲，令人幾悲吒。

Expressing my Inspiration in Twenty-three Poems, no.10

In simplicity, he left this world.
Meng Haoran is the one that I care.
Why need volumes of poems written?
With his verses, those of Bao and Xie
    fail to compare.
The same fish as before stays in the
    limpid river.
After the spring rain, there is more sugar
    canes to spare.
I heave sad sighs now and again
When at clouds of the southeast I stare.

遣興廿三首，其十一

我今日夜憂，諸弟各異方。不知死與
生，何況道路長。避寇一分散，飢寒
永相望。豈無柴門歸，欲出畏虎狼。
仰看雲中雁，禽鳥亦有行。

Expressing my Inspiration in Twenty-three Poems, no.11

My brothers live in different places.
These days I worry day and night.
I know not if they survive.
Worse still, they are far from this site.
Once we scatter fleeing from rebels,
In hunger and cold, forever we watch for
　　each other's sight.
Of course, we have a humble house to
　　return to.
Setting out on the path of tigers and
　　jackals gives me fright.
As I look up to wild geese in the clouds,
Even birds can form lines with their kin
　　in flight.

遣興廿三首，其十二

蓬生非無根，飄蕩隨高風。天寒落萬
里，不復歸本叢。客子念故宅，三年
門巷空。悵望但烽火，戎車滿關東。
生涯能幾何，常在羈旅中。

Expressing my Inspiration in Twenty-three Poems, no.12

Tumbleweeds are not without roots,
But get tossed as high winds blow,
Myriad miles away in the cold.
To rejoin their kind, they cannot go.
A wanderer thinks of his old home,
Deserted three years ago.
Depressed, I can see nothing but beacon
    fires.
East of the pass, full cart loads of
    soldiers and weapons follow.
How long can I really live,
So often trapped traveling to and fro?

遣興廿三首，其十三

昔在洛陽時，親友相追攀。送客東郊
道，遨遊宿南山。煙塵阻長河，樹羽
成皋閒。回首載酒地，豈無一日還。
丈夫貴壯健，慨戚非朱顏。

Expressing my Inspiration in Twenty-three Poems, no. 13

When I was in Luoyang years ago,
To relatives and friends, socially I relay.
Lodging by South Mountain, I rambled
And saw travelers off in the east
    outskirts on a pathway.
Dust and smoke block the long river.
Around Chenggao, soldiers with
    pennons make headway.
I recall the place where wine was plied.
To return, there should be a day.
A man values his strength and vigor.
Once distressed, my ruddy complexion
    cannot stay.

遣興廿三首，其十四

頗怪朝參懶，應耽野趣長。雨拋金鎖甲，苔臥綠沈槍。手自移蒲柳，家纔是稻粱。看君用幽意，白日到羲皇。

Expressing my Inspiration in Twenty-three Poems, no.14

I quite marvel at your loose attendance
    in the court.
It should be due to unconventional
    addictions you retain.
On the moss lies your green spear.
Your golden chain armor is thrown off
    in the rain.
You transplant rushes and willows.
There is just enough rice in the home
    you maintain.
As I watch you with a hermit's mind,
In broad daylight, you reach the age of
    simplicity in Fuxi's reign.

遣興廿三首，其十五

到此應常宿，相留可判年。蹉跎暮容色，悵望好林泉。何路沾微祿，歸山買薄田。斯遊恐不遂，把酒意茫然。

Expressing my Inspiration in Twenty-three Poems, no.15

The period of stay can well be a year.
One should come here and lodge often
    as a guest.
Sunset colors remind me of time
    wasted.
The fine forest and spring get me
    depressed.
Let me return to the hills and buy bare
    lots.
How do I live with a small salary
    possessed?
I suspect I will never finish the project.
With wine in hand, let me sort my brain
    to get it expressed.

遣興廿三首，其十六

下馬古戰場，四顧但茫然。風悲浮雲
去，黃葉墜我前。朽骨穴螻蟻，又為
蔓草纏。故老行嘆息，今人尚開邊。
漢虜互勝負，封疆不常全。安得廉頗
將，三軍同晏眠。

Expressing my Inspiration in Twenty-three Poems, no.16

From my horse, I got off on an old
    battlefield
Which looked blurry all the way.
Yellow leaves dropped before me.
In a cheerless wind, clouds drifted away.
Entangled by vines,
Rotten bones by ant nests lay.
This old man sighed as he walked.
Frontier expansions still go on today.
We and barbarians take turns to win.
Marked frontier lines cannot always stay.
How can we get a general like Lian Po,
So all soldiers can oversleep any day.

遣興廿三首，其十七

野寺垂楊裏，春畦亂水閒。美好多影
竹，花鳥不歸山。城郭終何事，風塵
豈駐顏。誰能共公子，薄暮欲俱還。

Expressing my Inspiration in Twenty-three Poems, no.17

Plots get overrun by spring floods,
With a nameless temple amid many a
　　hanging willow.
Birds do not return to the hills.
Pretty flowers set bamboos aglow.
What will happen to our walled city?
How can we stay young when dusty
　　winds of war blow?
Towards sunset, as my princely friend
　　wants to return,
Who would have the chance to follow?

遣興廿三首，其十八

豐年孰云遲，甘澤不在早。耕田秋雨
足，禾黍已影道。春苗九月交，顏色
同日老。勸汝衡門士，忽悲尚枯槁。
時來展材力，先後無醜好。但訝鹿皮
翁，忘機對芳草。

Expressing my Inspiration in Twenty-three Poems, no.18

It matters not if sweet rain comes early.
Who talks about a late harvest in a
　　bumper year?
Wheat and millet shine forth by the road.
When fields get fall rain in a full share.
By the ninth month, seedlings of spring
　　will mature.
On the same day and in the same color,
　　they appear.
Do not grieve over your shriveled state
　　of mind and being.
Let me advise recluses everywhere.
In due course, your talent will be put to

use,
Sooner or later, however foul or fair.
I am amazed only at the immortals
Who face fragrant herbs without any
worldly care,

遣興廿三首，其十九

天用莫如龍，有時繫扶桑。頓轡海徒
湧，神人身更長。性命苟不存，英雄
徒自強。吞聲勿復道，真宰意茫茫。

Expressing my Inspiration in Twenty-three Poems, no.19

Sometimes tied to a Fusang tree,
Dragons work best in the immortals'
terrain.
Fairies can lengthen their bodies.
Where they put a stop, flash floods
surge in vain.
To no avail, heroes goad themselves on,
For their existence may not remain.

The True Almighty is unpredictable,
Keep quiet and say nothing again.

遣興廿三首，其二十

地用千里馬，無良復誰記。此日千里
馬，追風可君意。君看渥窪種，態與
駑駘異。不雜蹄嚙閒，逍遙有能事。

Expressing my Inspiration in Twenty-three Poems, no.20

Horses work best in the mortals' land.
Who will remember them if they are
　　no good?
Today it covers a thousand miles,
Galloping in the wind to suit the
　　owner's mood.
Look at the rare breed of horses.
Above the base, weary kind, they have
　　always stood.
They trot with ease and in style
If they do not mix with the wild bunch,

in the same neighborhood.

遣興廿三首，其二十一

驥子好男兒，前年學語時。問知人客
姓，誦傳老夫詩。世亂憐渠小，家貧
仰母慈。鹿門攜不遂，雁足繫難期。

Expressing my Inspiration in Twenty-three Poems, no.21

Jizi, a fine boy,
Learned to speak two years ago.
He can recite this old man's poems.
About visitors' names, he asks so he
  would know.
In turmoil, I pity him being small.
On a kind mother in poverty, he has to
  rely.
I cannot bring him to my secluded
  place.
Letter tied to the feet of wild geese
  are hard to come by.

遣興廿三首，其二十二

高秋登寒山，西望馬邑州。降虜東擊
胡，壯健盡不留。穹廬莽牢落，上有
行雲愁。老弱苦道路，願聞甲兵休。
鄴中事反覆，死人積如丘。諸將已茅
土，載驅誰與謀。

Expressing my Inspiration in Twenty-three Poems, no.22

In cloudless fall, I climb a cold hill
And at Mayi Sandbar to the south, stare.
Our tribal allies strike at barbarians to
    the east.
No a single able-bodied foe do they
    spare.
In the vastness, nomad yurts like domes
    are secured.
Cheerless clouds move here and there.
The old and weak weep on the road,
Eager to know about the end of warfare.
The Siege of Ye was a reversal.
Like mounds, corpses pile up

everywhere.

All the generals have gotten fiefs.

For future planning, with whom can we
share?

遣興廿三首，其二十三

干戈猶未定，弟妹各何之。拭淚沾襟
血，梳頭滿面絲。地卑荒野大，天遠
暮江遲。衰疾那能久，應無見汝時。

Expressing my Inspiration in Twenty-three Poems, no.23

Where have my brothers and sisters
gone?

Wars still remain.

Blood from wiped tears stains my lapels.

All over my face is my combed hair,
silken and white.

The lowland is in a huge wilderness.

Over the river, the far sky is at belated
twilight.

Weak and sick, how can I last long?
I should not be able to see you all again.

螢火

幸因腐草出，敢近太陽飛。未足臨書
卷，時能點客衣。隨風隔幔小，帶雨
傍林微。十月清霜重，飄零何處歸。

Fireflies

By chance emerging from rotting weeds,
They do not dare get near the sun in
    flight.
At times, they look like dots on a
    traveler's robe,
Though for reading, not sufficiently
    bright.
Beyond drapes, in the wind they appear
    small.
By the grove, in the rain they are slight.
In the tenth month with heavy, clear
    frosts,

Where do they return, drifting from site to site?

園

仲夏流多水，清晨向小園。碧溪搖艇潤，朱果爛枝繁。始為江山靜，終防市井喧。畦蔬繞茅屋，自足媚盤餐。

Garden

In midsummer, rivers run deep.
I approach my little garden, early in the day.
The broad blue creek is fit for boating.
Dense crimson fruits on branches look bright.
I started to find quiet hills and rivers.
In the end, it was for keeping the din of markets away.
Garden vegetables in plots wind my thatched cottage,
Enough on plates to rouse my appetite.

早起

春來常早起，幽事頗相關。帖石防隤
岸，開林出遠山。一丘藏曲折，緩步
有躋攀。童僕來城市，瓶中得酒還。

Getting up Early

I often rise early in spring,
Mostly engaged in what hermits find
    delight.
Piled rocks prevent banks from falling.
Clearing trees in a grove lends the far
    hill's sight.
Curved trails lie hidden in a hill.
I walk slowly and reach a height.
Returning from the city market,
My servant boy has bought a jug of wine
    on site.

覃山人隱居

南極老人自有星，　北山移文誰勒銘。
徵君已去獨松菊，　哀壑無光留戶庭。
予見離亂不得已，　子知出處必須經。
高車駟馬帶傾覆，　悵望秋天虛翠屏。

The Hermitage of Recluse Tan

Like the Old Man of South Pole and the
　　Star, you are well known.
"North Mountain Proclamation" needs
　　to be engraved and shown.
Your house and yard remain; ravines
　　look cheerless and dark.
Summoned by the king, you left your
　　pine and chrysanthemum alone.
You know about the necessary ways to
　　advance your life.
Into wartime wanderings, I cannot help
　　being thrown.
I get depressed by the fall scenery, once
　　green now bare.
In a high post, one takes the risk of
　　being overthrown.

315

Note: "North Mountain Proclamation" is a satire written by Kong Zhigui (447-501) on a recluse who answered the king to serve.

屏跡三首，其一

衰年甘屏跡，幽事供高臥。鳥下竹根行，黿開萍葉過。年荒酒價乏，日併園疏課。猶酌甘泉歌，歌長擊樽破。

Hiding my Tracks, no.1

As I age and wane, I gladly hide my
    tracks.
Seclusion allows for sound sleep and
    rest.
A bird descends to bamboo roots to hop.
Amid clumps of duckweed, a turtle slips
    through.
The price of wine is beyond me, in a
    year of bad harvest.

In my long song, I tap on my jar and
    break it,
Still singing and drinking from a sweet
    spring for brew.

屏跡三首，其二

用拙存吾道，幽居近物情。桑麻深雨
露，燕雀半生成。村鼓時時急，漁舟
箇箇輕。杖藜從白首，心跡喜雙清。

Hiding my Tracks, no.2

I follow Tao Qian's "Ineptitude" to keep
    my way of life.
Living in seclusion bonds me with
    nature tight.
Mulberry and hemp flourish in rain and
    dew.
Swallow and sparrow reach halfway in
    maturity.
Beats of village drums always go fast.
Every fishing boat is light.

Let me lean on my cane with a head of
white hair,
Glad that both my mind and tracks show
purity.

屏跡三首，其三

晚起家何事，無營地轉幽。竹光團野
色，舍影漾江流。失學從兒懶，長貧
任婦愁。百年渾得醉，一月不梳頭。

Hiding my Tracks, no.3

I get up late for nothing at home.
Without a scurry, the place becomes
more quiet.
The reflection of my cottage ripples in
the river.
The outskirt's colors are zeroed in by
the willow's glare.
With no schooling, my son is allowed
to be lazy.
In our long-term poverty, I let my wife

fret.
May I get to be a hundred fully drunk
And for a whole month, excused from
combing my hair.

西閣口號呈元二十一

山木抱雲稠，寒江繞上頭。雪崖纔變
石，風幔不依樓。社稷堪流涕，安危
在運籌。看君話王室，感動幾銷憂。

An Impromptu Poem on West Pavilion, Presented to Yuan, the Twenty-first

Hillside trees look dense with clouds as
an overlay.
At a height, a winding stream flows on
a cold day.
The rocky cliff has just been cleared of
snow.
Inside the pavilion, drapes in the wind
are in disarray.

We should tear over our country.
Peace relies on the king's policy in play.
You spoke before me on the monarchy.
Your insight moved me and melted my
   worries away.

風雨看舟前落花戲為新句

江上人家桃樹枝，春寒細雨出疏籬。
影遭碧水潛勾引，風妒紅花卻倒吹。
吹花困癲傍舟楫，水光風力俱相怯。
赤憎輕薄遮入懷，珍重分明不來接。
濕久飛遲半欲高，縈沙惹草細於毛。

In a Rainstorm, Watching Flowers Falling before my Boat, I Playfully Make New Lines

Peach twigs of a riverside household
Jut out of sparse hedges in a spring
   drizzle in the cold.
Green waters covertly draw the

reflections in.

Envious of pink blooms, the wind blows them over.

By the boat's paddles, I stay mad about blown petals,

Fearful of the shimmer and a blast.

I really hate frivolous people using their bosoms as a cover

And will not touch them as an openly respected lover.

In delay, the much drenched petals want to climb.

Finer than hair and mixed with sand and grass, they hover.

暮秋枉裴道州手扎率爾遣興寄

I

久客多枉友朋書，素書一月凡一束。
虛名但蒙寒溫問，泛愛不救溝壑辱。

齒落未是無心人，舌存恥作窮途哭。
道州手札適復至，紙長要自三過讀。
盈把那須滄海珠，入懷本倚崑山玉。
撥棄潭州百斛酒，蕪沒瀟岸千株菊。
使我晝立煩兒孫，令我夜坐費燈燭。
憶子初尉永嘉去，紅顏白面花映肉。
軍符侯印取豈遲，紫燕綠耳行甚速。

II

聖朝尚飛戰鬥塵，濟世宜引英俊人，
黎元愁痛會蘇息，夷狄跋扈徒逡巡。
授鉞築壇聞意旨，頹綱漏網期彌綸。
郭欽上書見大計，劉毅答詔驚群臣。
他日更僕語不淺，明公論兵氣益振。
傾壺簫管黑白髮，儛劍霜雪吹青春。
宴筵曾語蘇季子，後來傑出云孫比。
茅齋定王城郭門，藥物楚老漁商市。
市北肩輿每聯袂，郭南抱甕亦隱几。
無數將軍西第成，早作丞相東山起。
烏雀苦肥秋粟菽，蛟龍欲蟄寒沙水。
天下鼓角何時休，陣前部曲終日死。

322

附書與裴因示蘇，此生已愧須人扶。
致君堯舜付公等，早據要路思捐軀。

In Late Autumn, Pei of Daozhou Favored me with a Letter which I, on an Impulse, Replied to Express my Inspiration, with a Copy Presented to Censor Su Huan

I

Friends often favor this long-term guest
  with their letters.
The volume is a bundle a month that I
  obtain.
I lack real fame but they ask about me.
Despite that, the insult of my dying in a
  ditch is certain.

I have lost my teeth but not my heart.
I can still speak but from weeping at
  crisis, I refrain.
A letter from Daozhou happened to
  arrive.
I read the long letter over and over again.

I do not need a handful of pearls from
  the gray sea.
My mind relies on true friendship like
  Mount Kunlun's jade.
Let the wine of Tanzhou in a hundred
  pots be trashed.
Let a thousand chrysanthemums by
  River Xiao fade.

By day I bother my son to help me stand.
I waste lamplight sitting at night.
As I recall, you went off as the sheriff of
  Yongjia,
With a ruddy, white face, like a flower
  lit bright.

Into your hands, tallies and chops of
  power quickly passed.
Like rare horses, Zi Yan and Lu Er, you
  moved fast.

II

Heroic, talented men should be recruited

to save the world.
Dusts of war still fly in our sage reign.
The sorrow and pain of commoners will
end.
The savage nomads will waver, with
nothing to gain.

I heard of the king's intent to send out a
general
And hope you will mend the net of
justice with a legal review.
Like Guo Qin, you will petition the
throne with a big plan.
Like Liu Yi, you will shock ministers by
telling the king what is true.

At the feast, we spoke of Su Qin.
Among his famous heirs, his distant
descendant is his match.
For medicine, this old man of Chu goes
to the fishermen's market.
In the city of Changsha, there is his
study covered with thatch.

In his palanquin, he takes me along,

north of the market.
He hugs a jug by a secluded table,
  south of the city.
Our generals build grand mansions, like
  those in West Luoyang.
Soon he should be a minister and rise
  from obscurity.

Like birds, base people fatten silly with
  harvested gains in fall.
With hibernating in cold water and sand,
  flood dragons go along.
When can war bugles and drums end in
  this world?
Casualties of troops happen all day long.

This poem is shown to Su and sent to
  Pei.
I feel shamed of my life, needing help
  from others today.
You are entrusted to bring about a wise
  reign like Yao and Shun.
Think of self-sacrifice in a powerful
  post on an early day.

季秋江村

喬木村墟古，疏籬野蔓懸。素琴將暇
日，白首望霜天。登俎黃柑重，支床
錦石圓。遠遊雖寂莫，難見此山川。

Late Autumn in a Riverside Village

Wild vines hang from sparse hedges.
This village with tall trees started years
    ago.
A white-haired man watches the frosty
    sky,
Plucking a plain zither to pass each
    leisurely day.
A round, variegated stone props my bed.
On a platter are mandarin oranges,
    heavy and yellow.
I find it rare to see such hill and river,
Though feeling lonely traveling far
    away.

野望

清秋望不極，迢遞起居陰。遠水兼天
淨，孤城隱霧深。葉稀風更落，山迴
日初沈。獨鶴歸何晚，昏鴉已滿林。

Looking out in the Wilds

In clear fall, I cannot gaze at infinity.
At a distance rise layered shadows.
The far horizon is clean and seamless.
Deep in mist, the lone town barely
    shows.
The sun has just set behind remote hills.
Fewer leaves remain as a wind blows.
How late the solitary crane returns!
Crowding the forest are dusk crows.

甘園

春日清江岸，千甘二頃園。青雲羞葉
密，白雪避花繁。結子隨邊使，開筒
近至尊。後於桃李熟，終得獻金門。

Mandarin Orange Orchard

Near the shore of a limpid river in spring,
In a two-acre orchard, a thousand trees
    with mandarin oranges grow.
Thick leaves put a cloudy sky to shame.
Dense white flowers beat snow.
These fruits will be near the king, once
    unpacked.
Behind a frontier envoy, in bamboo
    tubes they follow.
Ripening behind peaches and plums,
To the palace, they finally are the ones
    to go.

湖城東遇孟雲卿復歸劉顥宅宿宴飲散因爲醉歌

疾風吹塵暗河縣，　行子隔手不相見。
湖城城南一開眼，　駐馬偶識雲卿面。
向非劉顥為地主，　懶回鞭巒為高宴。
劉侯歎我攜客來，　置酒張燈促華饌。
且將款曲終今夕，　休語艱難尚酣戰。
照室紅爐簇曙花，　縈窗素月垂秋練。
天開地裂長安陌，　寒盡春生洛陽殿。
豈知驅車復同軌，　可惜刻漏隨更箭。
人生會合不可常，　庭樹雞鳴淚如霰。

Meeting Meng Yunqing East of Hucheng, then Going back to Liu Hao's House for a Feast and an Overnight Stay, I Wrote a Song of Drunkenness after the Drinking Ended

In this dark dusty county with a sharp
    blast on the river,
I cannot see a fellow traveler just inches
    away.

South of Hucheng, with open eyes,
I meet Yunqing by chance as I stop my
    horse to stay.

Were it not for Liu Hao, my host,
To return for a grand feast, I was not
    inclined.
Count Liu praised me for bringing a
    guest.
Under lamplight, we were well wined
    and dined.

Stop talks on hardships in current wars.
Share our intimate feelings through the
    night.
A red brazier lights up this room like
    clumps of dawn flowers.
The moon beyond the window in fall
    hangs its shiny, silken light.

Renewed Luoyang palaces are like
    cold winter becoming spring.
Changan streets saw earth-shaking
    warfare.
From different career paths, we stay

on the same track.
Like the clepsydra, we value the goals
    and time we share.

In life, people do not always meet.
As roosters crow in courtyard trees,
    our tears fall like sleet.

山舘

南國晝多霧，北風天正寒。路危行木
杪，身遠宿雲端。山鬼吹燈滅，廚人
語夜闌。雞鳴問前舘，世亂敢求安。

Mountain Inn

Days are mostly foggy in the south.
A north wind makes a cold day.
On a steep path, I walk next to treetops.
I lodge at clouds' end, being so far away.
People talk in the kitchen as the night
    wanes.
Blown by mountain spirits, the flame of

my lamp cannot stay.

As the rooster crows, I ask of the inn
ahead.

With unrests all over, I dare not expect
safety on the way.

雲安九日鄭十八攜酒陪諸公宴

寒花開已盡，菊蕊獨盈枝。舊摘人頻
異，輕香酒暫隨。地偏初衣裌，山擁
更登危。萬國皆戎馬，酣歌淚欲垂。

On the Double Ninth Day at Yunan, Zheng, the Eighteenth, Brings Wine to Accompany Various Gentlemen in a Feast

Flowering is over in the cold.

Only dense chrysanthemums on stems
come in sight.

Those who used to pluck them vary.

As wine, its fragrance is brief and slight.

In this remote spot, I begin to wear my

lined robe
And amid many hills, climb to a height.
I want to tear after much drinking and
  singing.
With war-horses everywhere, we are
  still engaged in fight.

千秋節有感，其一

自罷千秋節，頻傷八月來。先朝常宴
會，壯觀已塵埃。鳳紀編生日，龍池
塹劫灰。湘川新涕淚，秦樹遠樓臺。
寶鏡群臣得，金吾萬國囘。衢尊不重
飲，白首獨餘哀。

On the Thousand Autumns Festival, no.1

In the eighth month, after canceling the
  Thousand Autumns Festival,
I often feel pained on the former king's
  birthday.

There were frequent feasts in the former
    reign.
Like dust, spectacular events cannot stay.

Our empire follows Yellow Emperor's
    Phoenix Calendar.
In the dragon pond, like a kalpa's ash,
    war spoilage lay.
By River Xiang, I shed renewed tears.
Towers, terraces and trees of the capital
    are far away.

Officials get jeweled mirrors as awards.
Despite restrictions, I strive to return
    from anywhere far away.
White-haired, I am left with lingering
    sorrow.
Never again will I drink a toast by the
    imperial highway.

千秋節有感，其二

禦氣雲樓敞，含風彩杖高。仙人張內
樂，王母獻宮桃。羅襪紅蕖艷，金羈
白雪光。舞階銜壽酒，走索背秋毫。
聖主他年貴，邊心此日勞。桂江流向
北，滿眼送波濤。

On the Thousand Autumns Festival, no.2

His Majesty stood in his broad tower
   amid clouds.
Wind-swept, colored banners are at a
   height.
Like fairies, musicians play in the inner
   court.
Spirit Queen Mother presents magic
   peaches as a birthday rite.

Dancers move in their silk socks on
   pretty red lotus pads.
Like white snow, golden bridles look
   bright.

To toast longevity, performers with
  goblets climb stairs.
Funambulists step backwards on ropes,
  slim and tight.

Our sage ruler will earn esteem in future
  years.
At the frontier today, our troops are in a
  bitter fight.
River Gui flows to the north.
Billows come fully to my sight.

過故斛斯校書莊二首，其一

此老已云歿，鄰人嗟未休。竟無宣室
召，徒有茂陵求。妻子寄他食，園林
非昔遊。空堂繐帷在，浙浙野風秋。

Passing by the Estate of the Late Editor Husi, no.1

This old gentleman has passed away.
Your neighbors sigh again and again.

Summons to Xuanshi Hall recalled Jia
    Yi, but you had none.
Xiangru of Maoling was recognized, but
    your posthumous title was in vain.
Your wife and children boarded with
    others.
The former look of your garden and
    grove fails to remain.
Autumn winds in the wilds growl.
In the empty hall is still hung the funeral
    curtain.

過故斛斯校書莊二首，其二

燕入非旁舍，鷗歸祇故池。斷橋無復
板，臥柳自生枝。遂有山陽作，多慚
鮑叔知。素交零落盡，白首淚雙垂。

Passing by the Estate of the Late Editor Husi, no.2

Swallows choose to enter your house,
    not your neighbors'.

Gulls return only to former pools to stay.
There are no replacement planks for the
  broken bridge.
New shoots grow where fallen willows
  lay.
Like Bao Shuya, you understand me
  well, to my shame.
This is written after your death, like the
  Shanyang piece of yesterday.
White-haired, I let my tears fall.
All my genuine friends have passed
  away.

過宋員外之問舊莊

宋公舊池舘，零落守陽河。枉道祇從
入，吟詩許更過。淹留問耆老，寂寞
向山河。更識將軍樹，悲風日暮多。

Passing by the Former Estate of Lord Song Ziwen

The former pool and lodge of Lord Song,

By Mount Shouyang, has to be repaired
  yet.
I enter the estate by way of a detour,
Wishing to chant poems on a revisit I
  get.
I linger with questions for the elders,
Before river and hill, lonely and quiet.
I become aware of the general's tree
That stands against frequent cheerless
  winds at sunset.

贈陳二補闕

世儒多汩沒，夫子獨聲名。獻納開東
觀，君王問長卿。皁雕寒始急，天馬
老能行。自到青冥裏，休看白髮生。

Presented to Chen, the Second, Rectifier of Omissions

Scholars of the age mostly live in
  oblivion.
Only you retain your renown.

In the east temple, you first presented
  your memorial.
As a senior minister, you were consulted
  by the crown.
An old rare horse can still cover miles.
To begin to strike in haste, black
  condors in the cold are known.
My soul will go to the dark, unseen
  world.
Let me ignore any white hair shown.

贈高式顏

昔別是何處，相逢皆老夫。故人還寂
寞，削跡共艱虞。自失論文友，空知
賣酒壚。平生飛動意，見爾不能無。

Presented to Gao Shiyan

Where was it we parted some time ago?
We are both old men on meeting again.
My old friend is still lonely.
Hiding our tracks, in hardship we both

sustain.
I have lost a friend in discussing
  literature.
Efforts to find a wine shop are in vain.
My life-long heightened level of energy,
In your presence, will always remain.

貽阮隱居昉

陳留風俗衰，人物世不數。塞上得阮
生，迴繼先父祖。貧知靜者性，白益
毛髮古。車馬入鄰家，蓬篙翳環堵。
清詩近道要，識子用心苦。尋我草徑
微，褰裳蹋寒雨。更議居遠村，避喧
甘猛虎。足明箕穎客，榮貴如糞土。

Presented to Recluse Ruan Fang

Customs and habits of Chenliu have
  declined.
In this age, important people do not
  remain.

On the frontier, I found Mister Ruan
Who continues the legacy in the long
	genealogical chain.

The poor knows when to be quiet.
In seniority, old people do not take their
	fuller white hair in vain.
Horses and carriages enter your
	neighborhood.
Like a round wall, blocking weeds have
	lain.

Your refreshing poems are in the right
	direction.
I know about your hard work, to be
	certain.
You visited me along a vague, grassy
	path
And lifting your robe, treaded through
	cold rain.

Then you discussed living in a far
	village,
To bear with fierce tigers, for a quiet
	terrain.

It goes to show that for recluses like
    those at Ji and Ying,
Manure is like fame and gain.

贈翰林張四學士

翰林逼華蓋，鯨力破蒼溟。天上張公
子，宮中漢客星。賦詩拾翠殿，佐酒
望雲亭。紫誥仍兼錧，黃麻似六經。
內分金帶赤。恩與荔枝青。無復隨高
鳳，空餘泣聚螢。此生任春草，垂老
獨漂萍。儻憶山陽會，悲歌在一聽。

Presented to Zhang, the Fourth, Fellow of the Hanlin Academy

The Hanlin Academy is near the palace.
Like a whale, you can split the dark
    gray sea below.
Exalted as in Heaven, you are the son of
    an elite,
Close to the king, like the "Wandering

Star" of the Han palace we know.

In writing poems or holding wine parties,
To Shicui Hall or Wangyun Pavilion,
    you go.
You draft well-sealed, purple edicts,
In the style of the Six Classics, on hemp
    paper in yellow.

In the inner palace, you accept a gift of
    green lichees,
With a sash in red and gold, that the
    monarch plans to bestow.
I am left with weeping amid fireflies,
Bereft of a mentor, like a phoenix on a
    high branch, to follow.

Let this life go on like spring grass.
Let me age alone, like duckweeds that
    drift with the flow.
If perchance you recall our intellectual
    meeting like that at Shanyang,
May you listen for once to my song of
    sorrow.

答鄭十七郎一絕

雨後過畦潤，花殘步屐遲。把文驚小陸，好客見當時。

A Quatrain in Answer to Mister Zheng, the Seventeenth

After rain, I pass through wet plots.
Amid wilted flowers, my steps are slow.
Like that of Younger Lu, your fine
  writings shock me.
Like Dangshi, you are another kind host
  I know.

蒹葭

摧折不自守，秋風吹若何。暫時花戴雪，幾處葉沉波。體弱春風早，叢長夜露多。江湖後搖落，亦恐歲蹉跎。

Reeds and Rushes

How hard are fall winds blowing!
Unable to fend for themselves, they snap
    and break.
Here and there, their leaves sink amid
    waves.
For a while, blooms wear crowns that
    snowflakes make.
Their frail forms stand in the early
    spring breeze.
Of the heavy night dew, the long clumps
    partake.
They perish late on river and lake.
I doubt their worth in longevity as
    Heaven's mistake.

奉陪鄭駙馬韋曲二首，其一

韋曲花無賴，家家惱殺人。綠尊雖盡
日，白髮好禁春。石角鉤衣破，藤枝
刺眼新。何時占叢竹，頭戴小烏巾。

Respectfully Accompanying Imperial Son-in-law Zheng in Weiqu, no.1

From each home in Weiqu, showy
    flowers flirt.
To our extreme frustration and fancy,
    they play.
Though green goblets of wine can help
    me pass time,
A white-haired man wishes spring could
    stay.
Corners of rocks catch and tear my robe.
Vines poke me in the eye without delay.
With the headdress of a recluse, I spend
    time by bamboos,
But when is the day?

奉陪鄭駙馬韋曲二首，其二

野寺垂楊裏，春畦亂水閒。美花多映
竹，好鳥不歸山。城郭終何事，風塵
豈駐顏。誰能共公子，薄暮欲俱還。

Respectfully Accompanying Imperial Son-in-law Zheng in Weiqu, no.2

A nameless temple stands among
    drooping willows in spring,
By a plot crossed by many a rivulet.
On bamboos, pretty blooms often cast
    their glow.
Not returning to the hills, charming
    birds are set.
What will finally happen to our city?
To stay young in wars, how do we get?
Who can accompany the son of an elite,
To return together towards sunset?

暮歸

霜黃碧梧白鶴棲，城上擊柝復烏啼。
客子入門月皎皎，誰家擣練風淒淒。
南渡桂水闕舟楫，北歸秦川多鼓鞞。
年過半百不稱意，明日看雲還杖黎。

Returning at Twilight

Perching on a green firmiana with
    yellow frost is a white crane.
On the city wall with watch rattles,
    crows caw again.
A wanderer enters the gate under bright
    moonlight.
Which family is pounding silk in a
    cheerless wind tonight?
Frequent drum beats of war will be by
    Qin streams, on return to the north.
Without a boat and oars, my voyage
    south on River Gui is in vain.
My age is over fifty, but my wishes are
    not met.
Tomorrow let me watch clouds on a
    cane.

江漲

江發蠻夷漲，山添雨雪流。大聲吹地
轉，高浪蹴天浮。魚鱉爲人得，蛟龍
不自謀。輕帆好去便，吾道付滄州。

The River Floods over

The river floods where nomads reside.
To the hills is added freezing rain.
The loud wind is ground-sweeping.
The sky's height is where waves can
    attain.
People capture fish and turtles.
Flood dragons are not for me to gain.
It is fine to set out with my light sail,
On my way to the hermit's sylvan,
    waterside terrain.

天河

常時任顯晦，秋至輒分明。縱被微雲
掩，終能永夜清。含星動雙闕，伴月
落邊城。牛女年年渡，何曾風浪生.

River of Heaven

Usually it may be seen or hidden.
By fall, it can be extra bright.
Even if covered by thin clouds,
Eventually it is distinct all night.
The size impresses all behind double
    gates of the palace.
In a frontier town, it goes down with
    moonlight.
Each year, Cowherd and Weaving Maid
    cross the Milky Way.
Do wind and wave ever rise from the
    site?

送張十二參軍赴蜀因呈楊五侍禦

好去張公子，通家別恨添。兩行秦樹
直，萬點蜀山尖。禦史新驄馬，參軍
舊紫髯。皇華吾善處，於汝定無嫌。

Seeing off Adjutant Zhang, the Twelfth, on his Way to Shu, I Follow up by Showing it to Censor Yang, the Fifth

Goodbye, Your Honor Zhang.
Your leaving gives an old family friend
    more lament.
Countless hills of Shu have pointed tips.
Trees on both sides of the road in Qin
    are not bent.
In the past, a censor got a new rare horse.
An adjutant kept his purplish whiskers,
    as legends went.
In his glorious, splendid career, Yang
    treated me well.
For you, he will surely harbor no
    resentment.

別常徵君

兒扶猶杖策，臥病一秋強。白髮少新
洗，寒衣寬總長。故人憂見及，此別
淚相望。各逐萍流轉，來書細作行。

Seeing off Chang, Board Secretary of the Civil Service

I have been sick all autumn
And got propped by my son and a cane.
My winter robe is too large and long.
When newly washed, sparse white hair
    can remain.
My old friend got worried seeing me.
On parting, we gazed at each other with
    tears of pain.
Each of us will drift and spin like
    duckweeds.
In your letter, write small for more lines
    to gain.

送裴二虯作尉永嘉

孤嶼亭何處，天涯水氣中。故人官就
此，絕境興誰同。隱吏逢梅福，遊山
憶謝公。扁舟吾已僦，把釣待秋風。

Seeing off Pei Qiu, the Second, to Take his Post as Sheriff of Yongjia

Where is "Solitary Isle Pavilion',
Among water vapors at the far edge of
the sky?
Who will share your elation before
peerless scenery?
There your official duties will lie.
Mei Fu, a sheriff in history, became a
recluse and immortal.
With Xie Lingyun, your enjoyment of
hills will form a spiritual tie.
I have already rented a small boat.
With my fishing tackle, I wait for fall
winds to come by

秋日寄題鄭豎湖上亭三首，其二

新作湖邊宅，遠聞賓客過。自須開竹
徑，誰道避雲蘿。官序潘生拙，才名
賈傅多。舍舟應卜地，鄰接意如何。

Sent on an Autumn Day to Zheng Jian on his Pavilion by the Lake, no.2

To your new lakeside cottage,
I heard from afar guests went.
Who says you are a hermit behind
 clouds and vines?
An open path among bamboos you have
 lent.
Like Pan Yue, you claim ineptitude in
 your rank of office.
Like Jia Yi, you possess great talent.
Leaving my boat, I should choose a
 piece of land.
Would you mind taking me as your
 next-door resident?

寄賀蘭銛

朝野歡娛後，乾坤震蕩中。相隨萬里
日，總作白頭翁。歲晚仍分袂，江邊
更轉蓬。勿云俱異域，飲啄幾回同。

Sent to He Lanxian

After the joy shared by the whole nation,
An earth-shaking turmoil came in the
    king's reign.
We have become white-haired,
After days of traveling over endless
    miles in twain.
We parted near the end of the year.
By the river, I now wander like a
    tumbleweed again.
We have wined and dined together
    several times.
On strange lands, from mentioning it,
    please abstain.

放船

收帆下急水，卷幔逐回灘。江市戎戎
暗，山雲淰淰寒。荒林無徑入，獨鳥
怪人看。已泊城樓底，何曾夜色闌。

Setting out by Boat

We lower the sail and enter the rapid
   waters.
Drapes twirl as we follow the reflux tide
   wave tight.
Clouds look sluggish above hills in the
   cold.
The riverside market is not bright.
A solitary bird gets suspicious as we
   look it over.
There is no path to enter the forest in
   blight.
We have moored beneath the wall tower.
When will be the end of night?

戲贈閿鄉秦少府短歌

去年行宮當太白，朝回君是同舍客。
同心不減骨肉親，每語見許文章伯。
今日時清兩京道，相逢苦覺人情好。
昨夜邀歡樂更無，多才依舊能潦倒。

A Short Song Playfully Presented to Sheriff Qin of Wenxiang

At the war capital by Mount Taibai last
year.
Returning from the dawn court, we had
the same lodge to share.
You often spoke about my superior
writings.
Just like flesh and blood, we had mutual
regard and care.
Today, between the two capitals, peace
is in sight.
In our meeting, we both strongly feel
our bonding is tight.
A very talented person like you can be
decadent.
You were a happier guest than before in

a fun party last night.

病馬

乘爾亦已久，天寒關塞深。塵中老盡力，歲晚病傷心。毛骨豈殊眾，馴良猶至今。物微意不淺，感動一沈吟。

Sick Horse

You gave me rides for a long time,
Deep in the frontier passes in the chill.
You used all your body strength in the
    dust.
Late in the year, I am broken hearted
    you are ill.
Your pelt and bone do not stand out.
Even now, you are tame and well-bred
    still.
I am moved as I chant your praise.
Your frame is small, but your worth to
    me is like a hill.

越王樓歌

綿州州府何磊落，　顯慶年中越王作。
孤城西北起高樓，　碧瓦朱甍照城郭。
樓下長江百丈清，　山頭落日半輪明。
君王舊跡今人賞，　轉見千秋萬古情。

Song of the Tower of the Prince of Yue

In the Mianzhou county government,
　how well and open things go.
Built by the Prince of Yue, in the
　Xianqing years, long ago,
This high tower stands to the northwest
　of the lone city.
To the walls, green tiles and red rafters
　lend a glow.

At the foot of the tower, the long river
　is deep and clear.
On the hill, only half the setting sun can
　appear.
I look forward to the eternal affinity of
　the people,

For this relic of the prince that all hold
 dear.

獨立

空外一鷙鳥，河間雙白鷗。飄飄搏擊
便，容易往來遊。草露亦多濕，蛛絲
仍未收。天機近人事，獨立萬端憂。

Standing Alone

Paired white gulls glide above the river.
A single bird of prey waits beyond the
 skies.
It strikes readily while soaring,
Returning soon with ease as it flies.
The day is early with dew still on the
 grass.
With intact spider webs around, danger
 lies.
Heaven's scheme of things affects us.
I stand alone as my worry in countless
 ways multiplies.

石鏡

蜀王將此鏡，送死置空山。冥冥憐香
骨，提攜近玉顏。衆妃無復嘆，千騎
亦虛還。獨有傷心石，埋輪月宇閒。

Stone Mirror

A Shu king put this mirror in a deserted
 mound,
Partaking in his consort's funeral and
 having his feelings shown.
She could hold it near her jade-like face.
In dark solitude, it is piteous to abandon
 her fragrant bone.
All other palace ladies sighed no more.
A thousand carriages returned, save her
 alone.
Like a buried disc in the moonlit heaven,
It is a unique, heart-breaking stone.

日暮

牛羊下來久，各已閉柴門。風月自清
夜，江山非故園。石泉流暗壁，草露
滴秋根。頭白燈明裏，何須花燼繁。

Sundown

Cattle and sheep came down long ago.
Each family has closed its ramshackle
  door.
The river and hill here are not those of
  my hometown.
The clear night is windy with the moon
  aglow.
In fall, dews drip onto the grass and
  their roots.
Along a dark stone cliff, spring waters
  flow.
A white-haired man like me, under
  bright lamplight,
Does not need dense blooms that can
  burn any more.

晚晴

村晚驚風度，庭幽過雨沾。夕陽熏細
草，江色映疏簾。書亂誰能帙，杯乾
可自添。時聞有餘論，未怪老夫潛。

Sunlit twilight

Rain has passed and dampened my
    secluded yard.
A sudden wind sweeps through the
    village at night.
The river's colors reflect on my thin
    drapes.
Slender grasses may smolder in the
    sunlit twilight.
I can refill an empty cup myself.
Who can wrap my books so the order is
    right?
Often I hear about critiques.
None should blame this old man for
    keeping himself out of sight.

三絕句，其一

楸樹馨香倚釣磯，斬新花蕊未應飛。
不如醉裏風吹盡，可忍醒時雨打稀。

Three Quatrains, no.1

By my fishing jetty, the brand new
　　petals
Of the fragrant Catalpa tree should
　　remain.
I would rather get drunk as winds blow
　　them away
Than when sober, see them thinned
　　down by rain.

三絕句，其二

門外鸕鷀久不來，沙頭忽見眼相猜。
自今已後知人意，一日須來一百迴。

Three Quatrains, no.2

The cormorant outside my gate has long
   been away.
Suddenly on the sands, with suspicious
   eyes it comes to stay.
From now on, after knowing my mind,
It wants to return a hundred times a day.

三絕句，其三

無數春筍滿林生，柴門密掩斷人行。
會須上番看成竹，客至從嗔不出迎。

Three Quatrains, no.3

In the grove, countless bamboo shoots
   are found.
With my well-shut ramshackle gate, the
   place is out of bound.
Let my guests fret; I will not go out to
   greet them.
I should really watch bamboos sprouted

from the first round.

蕃劍

致此自僻遠，又非珠玉裝。如何有奇
怪，每夜吐光芒。虎氣必騰上，龍身
寧久藏。風塵苦未息，持汝奉明王。

Tibetan Sword

Not adorned with pearls or jade,
This sword came from a faraway site.
Somehow, something strange happens.
It emits a glow each night.
A tiger's energy must prompt it to
    rush forward.
How can a dragon stand being long out
    of sight?
The unending turmoil of war pains me.
Let me present it to the king, wise and
    bright.

寄高適

楚隔乾坤遠，難招病客魂。詩名惟我
共，世事與誰論。北闕更新主，南星
落故園。定知想見日，爛漫倒芳尊。

To Gao Shi

It is hard to summon a sick traveler's
　　soul.
From the rest of the world, Chu is far.
With whom can I discuss problems of
　　this world?
Your fame in poetry matches mine.
A new ruler has taken over at the
　　northern palace.
Falling in the former garden is a
　　southern star.
I surely know that when we meet,
We shall go all out for our cups of
　　fragrant wine.

示侄佐

多病秋風落，君來慰眼前。自聞茅屋
趣，只想竹林眠。滿谷山雲起，侵籬
澗水懸。嗣宗諸子姪，早覺仲容賢。

To my Nephew Zuo

I am often sick in this windy season.
You came to comfort me in fall.
I tell myself of the fun with a thatched
    cottage.
My only wish is to sleep in a bamboo
    grove after all.
Clouds rise and fully cover valleys and
    hills.
The swollen brook pushes my fence to
    be a waterfall.
Of all the children and nephews of Ruan
    Ji,
I knew early on that Zhongrong in
    morals stood tall.

可惜

花飛有底急，老去願春遲。可惜歡愉
地，都非少壯時。寬心應是酒，遣興
莫過詩。此意陶潛解，吾生後汝期。

To my Regret

What is the hurry for flowers to fly away?
Old, I wish spring could prolong its stay.
To my regret, places of entertainment
Match not what my younger self
　　experienced yesterday.
Only poetry can let me express my
　　inspiration.
Wine should let me relax in a way.
Tao Qian should know what I have in
　　mind.
I am a compatriot of his, born on a later
　　day.

向夕

畎畝孤城外，江村亂水中。深山催短
景，喬木易高風。鶴下雲汀近，雞棲
草屋同。琴書散明燭，長夜始堪終。

Towards Evening

Fields lie outside this lonely city.
Deep in the hills, there is brief sunlight.
Villages lie among a chaos of rivulets.
Trees catch winds easily at a height.
Cranes descend on a misty sandbar
　　nearby.
Chickens roost near my thatched cottage
　　on site.
My zither and books scatter around a
　　bright candle.
Only in this way can I pass each long
　　night.

漫成兩首，其一

野日荒荒白，春流泯泯清。渚蒲隨地
有，村徑逐門成。只作披衣慣，常從
漉酒生。眼前無俗物，多病也身輕。

Two Casual Compositions, no.1

The spring current is not fully limpid.
In the wilds, there is weak sunshine.
Reeds are everywhere on islets.
Village paths and doors are in line.
I am used to wear my robe untied,
Often spending my days with unfiltered
   wine.
Without trite and base things in view,
I feel light-bodied and fine.

漫成兩首，其二

江皋已仲春，花下復清晨。仰面貪看鳥，回頭錯應人。讀書難字過，對酒滿壺頻。近識峨眉老，知予懶是真。

Two Casual Compositions, no.2

Under flowers, it is another early dawn,
By the river, with spring days already
   half spent.
I tilt my head eagerly for birds.
To those behind me, my replies are
   wrongly sent.
I pass over hard words as I read.
Full pots of wine before me are frequent.
Of late, I got to know an elder from
   Emei
Who understands that I am by nature
   really indolent.

374

雙燕

旅食驚雙燕，銜泥入此堂。應同避燥
濕，且復過炎涼。養子風塵際，來時
道路長。今秋天地在，吾亦離殊方。

Two Swallows

Two swallows startle me as I eat on my
    trip.
With mud in their beaks, they enter the
    hall.
Dry or wet, hot or cold,
We should share the same experience
    after all.
They raise their young and journey here,
On long roads, with dusty winds that
    can run tall.
I too shall leave this strange land.
Heaven and Earth still remain this fall.

野望

清秋望不極，迢遞起層陰。遠水兼天
淨，孤城隱霧深。葉稀風更落，山廻
日初沈。獨鶴歸何晚，昏鴉已滿林。

View of the Wilds

In clear fall, I cannot catch sight of
  infinity.
The distant view is under layered
  shadows.
Water flows afar under a clear sky.
Hidden in deep fog, the lone city hardly
  shows.
More of the few remaining leaves drop
  in the wind.
Beyond remote hills, the setting sun
  goes.
How late the solitary crane returns!
The forest is already full of dusk crows.

哭李常侍嶧二首，其一

一代同流盡，修文地下深。斯人不重見，將老失知音。短日行梅嶺，寒山落桂林。長安若個畔，猶想映貂金。

Weeping for Li Yi, Imperial Attendant, no.1

The gallant man of a generation is gone.
The title of a literary man underground
  is yours firmly to hold.
This person will not be met again.
I have lost one who understands me,
  getting old.
On this short day, your casket passes
  Plum Ridge.
Roads at Guilin run under hills that
  look cold.
How many former companions of yours
  at Changan
Would still think of you, aglow with
  sable and gold?

哭李常侍嶧二首，其二

青瑣陪雙入，銅梁阻一辭。風塵逢我
地，江漢哭君時。次第尋書劄，呼兒
檢贈詩。發揮王子表，不愧史臣詞。

Weeping for Li Yi, Imperial Attendant, no.2

At Tongliang County, I was blocked
    from leaving.
Into the palace, I accompanied you in
    entry.
I weep for you at Yangzi and Han.
When we met, wind and dust ran free.
One by one, I look for your letters in a
    bundle
And call my son to search for poems
    you gave me.
The praise of palace historians on you
    will cause no shame.
In the detailed genealogy, you are a
    prince in the royal clan of Li.

畏人

早花隨處發，春鳥異方啼。萬里清江上，三年落日低。畏人成小築，褊性合幽棲。門逕從榛草，無心待馬蹄。

Wary of People

Spring birds call in a strange land.
Flowers open early wherever I go.
On myriad miles, above a limpid river,
For three years, the dusk sun hangs low.
I built a small hut to distance people.
A secluded way of life I naturally follow.
I am not inclined to wait for visitors.
On the path to my house, let weeds grow.

秋野五首，其一

秋野日疏蕪，寒江動碧虛。繫舟蠻井絡，卜宅楚村墟。棗熟從人打，葵荒欲自鋤。盤飧老夫食，分減及溪魚。

The Wilds in Fall, no.1

The cold river ripples the reflected blue
  void.
The wilds in fall each day look more
  worn and bare.
I tie my boat in wild Shu, the domain
  under the Well Star
And build a hut by the village market
  square.
I want to dig the wilting mallows myself.
About someone knocking ripe dates off
  my tree, I do not care.
A portion of my meal is taken out
For the fish in the brook to share.

秋野五首，其二

意識浮生理，難教一物違。水深魚極
樂，林茂鳥知歸。衰老甘貧病，榮華
有是非。秋風吹几杖，不厭北山薇。

The Wilds in Fall, no.2

It is easy to recognize the rules of an
    impermanent life,
But hard to make one forego one's
    birthright.
Birds know when to return to dense
    forests.
In deep water, fish take extreme delight.
I accept poverty and illness as I age.
With glory comes the need to discern
    what is wrong or right.
A fall wind blows on my table and cane.
At North Mount for recluses, a diet on
    vetches is alright.

秋野五首，其三

禮樂攻吾短，山林引興長。掉頭紗帽
側，曝背竹書光。風落收松子，天寒
割蜜房。稀疏小紅翠，駐屐近微香。

The Wilds in Fall, no.3

Rite and music help me attack my
   shortcomings.
Hill and forest rouse my interest that can
   last.
I sun my back with light on bamboos
   and books.
On my turned head, the gauze hat
   becomes aslant.
Cut honeycombs off on cold days.
Collect pine cones that drop in a blast.
I stop and get close to the few flowers
That look small and smell faintly
   fragrant.

秋野五首，其四

遠岸秋沙白，連山晚照紅。潛鱗輸駭
浪，歸翼會高風。砧響家家發，樵聲
箇箇同。飛霜任青女，賜被隔南宮。

The Wilds in Fall, no.4

In fall, with white sand on distant shores,
Linked hills at night look red aglow.
Homebound birds catch tall winds.
Submerged fish escape from each
  fearful billow.
Sounds of mallets come from every
  family.
In the same pitch, beats of woodcutting
  go.
Frost Goddess dictates the release of
  frost.
Her quilt is not what I got from South
  Palace long ago.

秋野五首，其五

身許麒麟畫，年衰鴛鴦群。大江秋易
盛，空峽夜多聞。徑隱千重石，帆留
一片雲。兒童解蠻語，不必作參軍。

The Wilds in Fall, no.5

Wish I had my portrait in the palace
Unicorn Hall of Fame.
Old, among mandarin ducks, not court
officials, I appear.
The big river rises easily in fall.
In the deserted gorge, night noises I
often hear.
A swathe of clouds remains on my sail.
Countless layers of rocks make the path
unclear.
My son understands nomad dialects.
It may not lead to a high post, like an
adjutant, in his career.

李司馬橋了承高使者自成都回

向來江上手紛紛，三日成功事出群。
已傳童子騎青竹，總擬橋東待使君。

With the Bridge of Adjutant Li Completed, Governor Gao is Returning to Chengdu

Of late by the river, builders work hard
    in each case.
The uncommon project was done in just
    three days.
All plan to wait for the governor east of
    the bridge,
With children on green bamboo horses,
    already the rumor says.

營屋

我在隱江村，能令朱夏寒。陰道積水
內，高入浮雲端。甚疑鬼物憑，不顧
剪伐殘。東偏若面勢，戶牖永可安。
愛惜已六載，茲晨去千竿。蕭蕭見白
日，洶洶開奔湍。度堂匪華麗，養拙
異考槃。草茅雖薙葺，衰疾方少寬。

洗然順所適，此足代加餐。寂無斤斧
響，庶逐憩息歡。

Working on the House

I have shade in my riverside village
That chills me in summer with heat at its
    height.
Their shadows get into deep waters.
At the edge of drifting clouds, their
    tallness comes in sight.
I much suspected goblins lying there
    in wait
And chose to chop them down outright.
I have loved and valued them for six
    years.
This morn I got rid of a thousand
    bamboo canes.
That opens up the view of a rapid river
And in the whistling wind, brings strong
    sunlight.
I did not plan on a grandiose hall.
Mine is for practicing "Ineptitude", not
    a recluse's site.
Couch grass has been cut for thatching.

My relief from aging and illness is
　　slight.
It is enough to replace eating more
When I follow freely what is right.
It is silent without the sound of the axe.
I hope for resting in delight.

琴臺

茂陵多病後，尚愛卓文君。酒肆人間
世，琴臺日暮雲。野花留寶靨，蔓草
見羅裙。歸鳳求凰意，寥寥不復聞。

The Zither Terrace

After a prolonged illness at Mouling,
He kept his love for Zhuo Wenjun on
　　his mind.
Their tavern was part of the mortal
　　world.
The Zither Terrace went to clouds at
　　sunset.
We can see her silk skirt among rank

grass.

Wild flowers remind us of her precious dimples left behind.

Like a male phoenix returning to seek his mate,

He did not let his wish be heard and all is quiet.

沙鷗：杜甫詩集

陳鈞洪譯